Frederick H Pratt and Son

Complete Cycle Engineers

Author: Alvin J E Smith

Member: Veteran-Cycle Club

The John Pinkerton Memorial Publishing Fund

Following the untimely death of John Pinkerton in 2002, a proposal was made to set up a fund in his memory.

The objective of the Fund is to continue the publishing activities initiated by John Pinkerton, that is to publish historical material on the development of the bicycle of all types and related activities. This will include reprints of significant cycling journal articles, manufacturers' technical information including catalogues, parts lists, drawings and other technical information.

Published by the John Pinkerton Memorial Publishing Fund, 2006
© John Pinkerton Memorial Publishing Fund 2006. All rights reserved.

ISBN 978-0-9552115-3-9

Printed by Quorum Print Services Ltd. Cheltenham. December 2006

Cover pictures: On the left Peter Tester, FHP's frame builder, on the right Noel Pratt, son of Frederick Pratt. Coloured illustration is of early head badge transfer.

The coloured picture on the back cover is of Joan, Fred and a visitor in front of the shop

JPMPF Publications

Lightweight Cycle Catalogue Volume 1

An Encyclopaedia of Cycle Manufacturers - compiled by Ray Miller

Frederick H Pratt and Sons - Complete Cycle Engineers - Alvin J E Smith

The Electric-Powered Bicycle Lamp 1888-1948 - Peter W Card

All publications are available through the Veteran-Cycle Club sale officer.

Contents

Contents ·· 3
Foreword ·· 5
Introduction ··· 7
Early Days ·· 9
Working for the Claud Butler Company ······················ 11
A Time for Change ··· 14
The Shop ·· 15
Fred and the Shop ··· 17
The "Jack Knife" ·· 19
Purpose of the Leaflets ··································· 23
The Later Frames ·· 25
Working in the Shop ······································· 31
Bikes and their Riders – Owners Anecdotes and Stories ····· 36
Concluding Remarks ·· 39
Appendix A ·· 41
Appendix B ·· 45
Appendix C The Leaflets ··································· 49

Foreword

When Frederick Pratt opened his cycle shop in Salfords in 1948 this section of the London to Brighton road was already a racing Mecca for South London cyclists. My first two 25 mile time-trials were on this G9 course, coincidentally in 1948, but I must confess to never owning a Frederick, although my husband John bought a Claud from them and our sons were kitted out with stock bikes. We became good friends with both Joan and Fred over the years and always received a warm welcome. As Alvin records, most clubs had their favoured local dealer/frame builder in that period and Pratts mainly drew their lightweight custom from the Redhill and Crawley clubs. I note too quite a few familiar Kingston Phoenix RC names in Table A.1. Other folk would always 'drop in' to the shop for spares on a Sunday morning, and as Noel rightly claimed, in later years it was for something desperately needed to restore an old machine long since out of production. Thanks, Noel, you so frequently were able to come up with the goods.

It is important that the history of the smaller cycle manufacturers who helped make our sport is recorded, and Alvin Smith has helped to achieve this. Those of us who personally knew the Pratt family will instantly recognize and recall Fred, Joan, and Noel and let us not that Joan like her brothers Claud and Geoffrey was a Butler.

Chris Watts.

Addiscombe CC and RTTC District Secretary.

Acknowledgements

The following people have all been very helpful with their comments on my text, and in many cases, have contributed enormously with comments or their detailed recollections and in some cases with their photographic records. Nevertheless if there are any innaccuracies they are mine and I shall br happy to amend them if future editions allow

Their kind assistance and enthusiastic responses are gratefully acknowledged.

Malcolm Bainbridge, Gordon Ball, Ken Bean, Geoff Boxall, Cally Calloman, Peter Crowsley, Clive Cruttendon, Pat Curtis, John Eglington, Graham Haysom, Colin Heath, Janet & Stuart Hoare, Jim Hollands, Pat Illing, Tony Killick, Harry Knowles, Tom Lane, Colin Matthews, Clive Oxx, Malcolm Pink, Betty & Noel Pratt, Jonathan Spearman-Oxx, Brenda & Peter Tester, Chris Watts, John Wolfson

Alvin Smith, 11/8/2006

Introduction

Frederick H Pratt & Son, was the name above the only cycle shop in Salfords, Surrey. The shop opened for business just a few years after the Second World War but sadly closed forever in January 2003. The shop was on the A23 main road about three miles south of Redhill, and thus had served the locality well for almost fifty five years. The shop can be seen enjoying the quietness of the 1950's in Figure 1.

Figure 1 *The shop can be seen as the third premises from the right with its light blue painted window surround*

The shop was known to keen cyclists far beyond its immediate environs as demonstrated by the fact that a visiting Mancunian cyclist could write " it was specially agreeable to cyclists using the famous A23 – to see a bright cycle shop made even more eye catching by slogans extolling our pastime"[1].

This account is the tale of three men : the firm was the fruits of one man's early labours and experience; was almost the entire working life of the second man in the story; and was a major part of a third, the quiet man of the trio. The two main men were of course Frederick Herbert Pratt and his son, Philip Noel Pratt. The third was Peter Tester, the firm's loyal and self effacing frame builder.

Mr Pratt senior, Fred Pratt, died in 1967. However, his reputation as a charismatic enthusiast lived on in his shop. He was a man who had held strong opinions – and who liked to expand upon them, but above all, he was a man who lived for cycling and all it involved. Figure 2 shows Fred Pratt as he might well have wished to be remembered, on a bike of his own making. Note, however that this Lilliputian machine would have been made when he worked for Claud Butler.

Figure 2 *Fred going for a ride!*

Noel, as he is always known, took over the mantle left by his father and brought his own characteristics, an infectious laugh and a similar, though differing, idiosyncratic approach to bike shop management. People who knew both Fred and Noel, say that Noel is a real chip off the old block.

This history has only been possible by pestering Noel and a few old friends for the story. It is focused on the works of the founder, Fred, and Noel, his successor, with reminiscences by Pete and a number of others, many of who never stopped being enthusiastic supporters of the firm. In addition, the firm always enjoyed a loyal 'entourage' of riders, many from the Redhill Cycling Club (RCC) as well as numerous local inhabitants who brought their sick and poorly bikes to be made whole again. Last but not least, and central to the story of the firm, and its operation, was the irrepressible matriarch, Mrs. Joan Mary Pratt.

Reader, if when reading this story, the bicycling content seems to stray, remember if you will that this story is for those who wish to remember the Pratt shop and family as well as the cycle historian. In the account I have tried to bring out the essential 'family' aspects that typify the FHP & Son concern and because of the families connection, some that touch on the Butler clan. The photographs presented have very kindly been made available by Noel, and illustrate the family as a background to the main story.

8

Early days

Frederick Pratt, or Fred as he was universally known, was born in Wimbledon on 25 April 1904, and lived as a child in 3 Herbert Villas, Herbert Road. His wife, Joan had been born a few years later (23 October 1910) and lived as a child at 11 Gladstone Road, Wimbledon. Joan was born Joan Mary Butler, and was the younger sister of Claud Butler. Now of course Claud Butler is a name of renown in the cycling world, but back then he was just a young man. Joan first met Fred as a school-friend of her brother. How the adult romance started is not known, but, supposing it was not a continual friendship, it seems likely to have been re-kindled through meeting each other in the Claud Butler cycle shop. In the story hereafter, the Claud Butler firm, the experience of which was so formative for Fred, is simply referred to as CB or CBs. One photograph I have been passed (Figure 3) shows Claud Butler's father taken some time in the 1920's – perhaps just outside his son's then newly established shop in East Hill Wandsworth?

Figure 3 Claud Butler senior 1920's

Joan and Frederick had been childhood sweethearts since Joan was nine - as she was happy to tell you at any time, in between making sure the shop's cats didn't need feeding. Joan had been born with a brittle bone condition. Although as a child she ran about with the others, she was always prone to bone breakages. Shortly after her seventh birthday, she became confined to a wheelchair after which she gradually lost the use of her legs and was wheelchair bound throughout her adult life. But she had had those early years and one of her strongest and fondest memories was "of the rustle and feel of crisp autumn leaves against my bare legs when running through the woods as a young girl". There was no other infirmity about Joan and apart from her physical incapacity she enjoyed life to the full- and instructed others in it, as Noel still recalls, a little ruefully at times.

Fred Pratt's first job, and Noel thinks his first love - because of the way it guided his life - was as an assistant to a landscaping contractor. Noel recalls how his father really enjoyed landscaping and working with plants in their various gardens, and his inclination to a clear line and good design carried over from the garden to the family house and to his bicycles. Fred was a well built, strapping young man but his first career came to an end in the early 1920's – the years leading to the Depression. The work the landscaping firm had been carrying out on an estate was very nearly completed, when the boss suddenly sacked Fred, ostensibly because he was caught smoking during a lull in activities. The sacking was felt to be canniness on the part of the boss, who had no other work in sight after the current job and wanted rid of his employee.

With little employment about, Fred was lucky to find work with the Surbiton Fire Brigade. Figure 4 shows Fred proudly showing off his uniform in the mid 1920's.

How much Fred enjoyed this work is not recorded, but he was soon offered rather more enticing work. This invitation came perhaps out of the blue from his old school and family friend, Claud Butler.

Figure 4 Fred Pratt as a Fireman at Surbiton circa 1926

Claud Butler, and in particular his cycle shops, form an important though largely a background part to this story because of the family connections but more importantly because of the excellent training that Fred Pratt acquired during his time with CBs and possibly his reaction to it. It is clear that all the Butler family shared the drive and panache that would make CBs such a power in the cycling world by the 1930's. Joan's education was fragmentary, because, due to her health, the authorities had classified her as disabled. She was consequently not allowed to attend school. Instead her mother brought her up at home. Joan, who was always a voracious reader, effectively helped herself to her learning, and as an independent young lady taught herself to type. She then busied herself with voluntary administrative work for the local Girl Guides from her home and occasionally from a hospital bed. The Guides reciprocated of course, and took her, to her great delight, on

Early days

some of their outings. She was never so happy as when out and about doing things with other people.

Claud's first shop opened in East Hill, Wandsworth, in 1928 though it was not long before the office moved to Clapham Manor Street, South London, where later the main factory was sited. It was no surprise that Claud's mother, who was always known as Ma, even in the wider Pratt part of the Butler Family, was initially the chief accountant.

Figure 5 CB's mother seen in the 1930s with her daughter Joan Pratt and one of her other granddaughters

Noel is always happy to recount the story, of how Mrs Butler Senior used to take the takings home from the shop in a carrier bag loosely held in her hand, while her smart handbag, which was conspicuously held very tightly under her arm, had no money in it. One evening she was attacked just as she left the shop just before closing one night. The thieves snatched her handbag, but left her with the carrier bag with the money. Fred and members of the staff sallied forth and had a right old fisty cuffs with the attackers who then ran off – as it happens with nothing. It was one of Fred's stories that he was quite upset that they gave in so easily as he felt he was just getting warmed up when they escaped.

Of course the young Joan was often to be found in her brother's shop, or more likely behind the shop, because she rapidly became a dab hand at the initial lacing up of wheels. Fred was the first outsider to be invited to join Claud's new venture, and started with CBs on the very first day. It may have been here that the romance between Fred and Joan blossomed. Was it to be with Joan, or to be a part of the cycling world, that was the initial enticement for Fred to join CBs?

One of the reasons for – but also one of the key pleasures of writing an account like this is to be able to present to readers items that they might never otherwise see. This seems a good place therefore, with Noel's permission, to include Figure 6 which is a water colour sketch of Claud done by Joan in her own drawing album, (do you remember them?) in or about 1942.

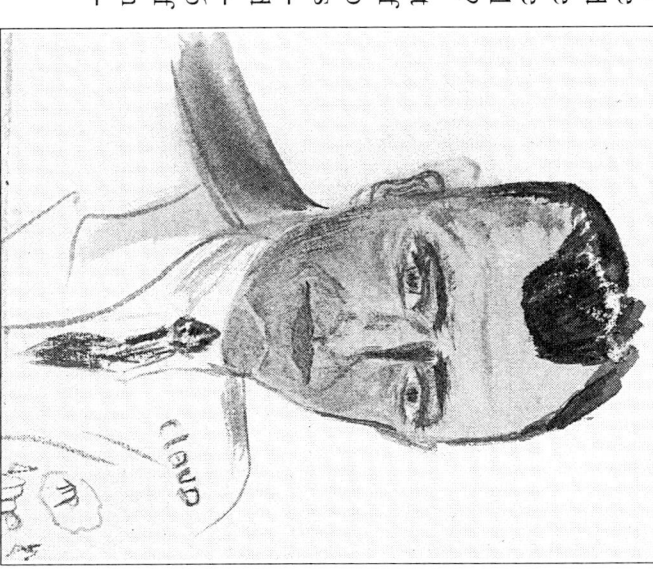

Figure 6 Claud Butler drawn by an adoring sister, Joan Pratt

Working in the Claud Butler company

Doubtless Fred had learnt to be handy with metal working tools during his time at the Fire Brigade, but certainly having joined CBs, it was not long before he was a trained cycle mechanic and a valued frame builder for Claud's young firm. Fred would have enjoyed the doubtless exciting times of the late 1920's and early 1930's as the English lightweight movement became more commercially important and it became more imperative to have an 'angle' to obtain a competitive edge. Talking of competition – the lads at CBs were young and active and all sorts of cycle sport became their way. The photograph as Figure 7 shows Fred with others from CB sometime in the early days of the firm.

Noel considers that it was in this atmosphere that his father first got the bug for bicycle design and began to formulate his own principles of cycling and frame design, later to bloom in a most unusual way. Working with CBs, and being close to the centre of that little world, must have been like living in a hot house of ideas, both quirky and not so quirky. Noel got to know his father well, and says that his father had always enjoyed his eleven mile ride to and from work to his home in Tolworth. Noels feels that the thinking behind Fred's activities was mainly done on these rides. Certainly Noel remembers that on arriving home at night his father was prone to dash into the house to set down on paper what he had been thinking about on his ride. CBs wanted to be up there with the continental makers and ahead of the other UK market leaders and Fred became either one of, or perhaps, the designer of frames for CBs. The 1936 CB ultra short wheel base (USWB) tandem was a real market leader - just look at how many survive today. This design, which Fred developed for CBs – though almost certainly with some help from the pre-existing and very similar Selbach product – immediately prior to the 1936 debut, is shown in Figure 8 taken from the Pratt family photo album.

The design was claimed as a first by the firm despite the Selbach claims. The CB's catalogue of 1939 shows a patent number issued to the fully described CB USWB system. The USWB tandem probably helped CBs to survive the low times in the 1930's. Whatever and wherever the origin of the idea, Noel Pratt knows that the detailed design of the handsome CB bottom bracket casting on the CB USWB machines,

Figure 7. Frederick Pratt on the right with the Claud Butler "A" cycle polo team in the 1920's

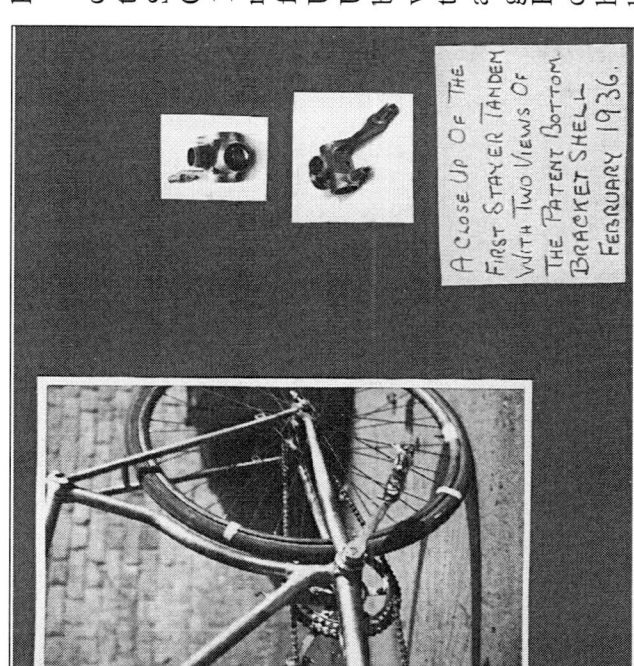

Figure 8. The Claud Butler USWB tandem rear bracket – designed by Fred Pratt

Working in the Claud Butler company

the strength of which gave the CB frame its delightful elegance and undoubted stiffness, was his father's work.

Noel remembers his father reminiscing, although this would have been very much later in his father's own shop, about the heated discussions over the development work that had gone into the design of the lugs and castings. In particular, he remembers how Fred would revive for his listeners the indignation he felt when Claud once told him that he spent far too long on the drawing board and should get on with more productive work. Mind you, the story always ended with Fred remembering that Claud did later acknowledge the great importance of the tandem, and how it had saved the firm's cash flow with its phenomenal success, and how Fred's work had been invaluable in obtaining the patent for the frame design.

It may also have been Fred's detailing that produced some of the classic curly cut out lugs that were to become such a feature of top quality lugged CB bikes. These lugs were so visually attractive that, to quote Noel's flowery (perhaps culinary!) phrase, "you could always tell a CB frame, no matter how much strawberry jam paint had been applied by subsequent owners."

Fred was undoubtedly a key and trusted frame builder with CBs, being the sole builder of the CB frames used for the famous first ever six day race at Olympia in 1936. The team won and the ensuing publicity, milked as hard as possible by the astute Claud of course, was one of the best publicity advantages the CB firm ever had. Most CB advertisements, and certainly those in 19392 emphasised a sporting design of frame with steep angles and responsive steering. It may have been about this time that Fred's ideas began to diverge from CBs mainstream and largely competition driven approach. Noel remembers that his father was affronted by the steep angles of the track frames he had been instructed to build at the Herne Hill shop and deplored the commercial trend of using such frame designs to sell to fashion conscious but in his view technically ignorant club and high-street shoppers. But more on this aspect later, as it is a key issue in relation to one model of the Frederick bicycle.

It is only fair to record here that CBs did of course offer less severe angled frames in the complete range of bikes that the firm made. Doubtless Fred's contribution to these less racy machines was also important to the firm. It is not possible now to know how much Fred, who was at one time CB's Chief Engineer, was personally involved in the production of such CB classics as the trikes, tandem trikes and other exotica such as the miniature bikes made for circus and stage acts. Certainly when it came to carefully constructed one offs Fred was your man, and he was very proud to be able to help handicapped riders – one example for the family archive is seen in Figure 9.

Of course CBs did at this time employ a number of frame builders who like Fred, had started as youngsters. Many keen young cyclists were taken on as filers, devel-

Figure 9. Details of a special CB tricycle made by Fred

oped their skills and went on to be their own masters. Such famous names include Les Ephgrave, Fred Dean, Bill Phillbrock, and George Stratton, to name a few. George would end up taking over the remains of the CB workshops, selling his bikes as George Stratton's, though at least initially they were thinly disguised CBs in style.

During the war CBs were of course occupied with war work, and had War Department contracts given to them. An important job Fred undertook for CBs was the design of a folding bike for paratroopers to use. This had a special hinge near the bottom bracket and on the top tube. The bike design was said to have been technical approved by the War Ministry staff as it was a strong and simple design but Claud, when enquiring about the bid, was told that it had not been tendered in time, and so could not be considered. Strangely, BSA was already tooling up for their de-

Working in the Claud Butler company

sign which became the well known paratrooper folder just as the CB submission went in. It will perhaps be no surprise that Sir Bernard Docker, MD of the BSA, Sunbeam, Matchless, Daimler combine, was an adviser to the War Ministry at that time? Noel also remembers talk about a 'hush hush' folding radar aerial, which Fred designed, and which CBs made to fit under the canvas of open-top lorries so that it could be used covertly. At that time it was of course very innovatory, but whether it was ever put into production and use is by the nature of such items simply not known.

A time for change

After the war things were slow to return to normal due to all sorts of industrial shortages, but there were rumblings in the CB world. Claud's first marriage broke up and he remarried. The probable cause of his difficulties was a certain inattention to income and expenditure balances, and Ma had long since retired from the CB firm by then. Additionally there were the high costs of other aspects of Claud's flamboyant, not to say bacchanalian, life style. The difficulties were aided by a lack of concentration shown by Claud at this time, and no advice from the family or his managers seemed to have any effect. One of Noel's illuminating comments about this period is "when Claud went out of control." Fred was not the only member of the CB entourage who was unsettled at this time. Claud's younger brother, Geoffrey who had been a loyal member of the CBs workforce, decided he could do better elsewhere and left to set up his own cycle business, this time in Croydon.

We don't know a great deal about what precisely influenced Fred's attitudes to cycling in the prewar period, but he was a keen CTC supporter and he enjoyed his daily cycle ride of eleven miles to Clapham Manor Street. Noel knows his father was a keen supporter of the Tooting Bec Club, and had raced with them in his youth. He was, however, despite being very busy with the demands of the expanding CB empire, devoted to his young wife Joan, and in due course to a young family. Looking after Joan and, when he was born Noel, who was also delicate as a youngster, must have taken up a great deal of his energies.

The pressures on Fred must have been great as Joan's life as a young mother was complicated by her physical handicaps, and in his absence she was effectively housebound. Noel was born on 18 April 1932. His birth had been a traumatic period for his parents, as he had been one of a pair of twins. His twin sister had died in childbirth. His mother had never told him, and Fred, who in later life became a Christian Scientist, may have been convinced in his beliefs during this period of their lives. For Noel however it was a peaceful upbringing in the late 1930's even though for the adults it was an unsettling time. Figure 10 shows Noel just before the war in the back garden of their home.

After the war, perhaps Fred felt he had seen the best of CBs. Perhaps also, reacting to his own feelings and to the pressing needs of his family at this time, he decided he had seen the writing on the wall – but whatever it was that drove him, - it was time to go!

Figure 10   Noel Pratt proud owner of his Vauxhall 30/98 ! Aged 3 years in 1935

The shop

The family firm of Frederick H Pratt and Son, Complete Cycle Engineers opened in Salfords on 19 July 1948. Note that telling phrase - 'Complete Cycle Engineers'. Fred was really proud, particularly as a self-taught man, of the skills that he had acquired and then demonstrated by all the design work and one-off's for which he had been responsible when working with CBs.

The shop was in the main shopping area of Salfords. As could be seen in Figure 1 the shop stood back from the busy A23 road on a service road running parallel to the busy main road. Before the M23 was built in the 1970's this road was a really busy national thoroughfare, being the direct road from London to Brighton.

Noel recalls, from nearly fifty five years distance in time, the turmoil of the early days at the new shop, enlarging the ground floor shop area so that his mother could access all the shelves and thereby serve the customers, and he and his father engineering the lift shaft installation. And after that, there was the work of clearing out the builders' rubbish from the area behind the shop, and setting up the new workshop there.

The shop also provided a three storey home. The ground floor had already had a small shop, and there was enough garden to put up a good workshop. Fred, ever the practical mechanic, installed a special lift in the premises with his own design of hand wound mechanism to raise and lower the lift. The lift should have allowed Joan to leave the upstairs family home more independently but was not a success. Noel recalls that, though the hatch-way for the lift remained in place until the recent closing of the shop, his mother never liked the hand driven arrangements. Fred soon gave in, and the mechanical parts were dismantled. From that time on Fred carried Joan up and down the stairs everyday.

The premises, although now in the middle of a parade of shops, was when opened an end-of-terrace shop and there were long family debates as whether or not to buy the adjacent plot of land. At £200 it can be seen now as a snip, but then it was unfortunately a step too far for Fred who was already financially stretched with the mortgage on the shop. Figure 11 shows the shop from the pavement on the A23 with Joan and Fred in front of the window, taken probably about 1948.

Joan soon found her wheels so to speak and was to be a 'god-send' in the shop. She thoroughly enjoyed the hustle and bustle and, ironically, seldom seemed to feel the urge to leave it and explore the flat area around Salfords that had been one of the main reasons for the original choice for the shop's location.

Fred and Joan's friends from the south London days soon found them and Figure 12 shows Joan with Evelyn Hamilton, who was a CB sponsored rider and family friend, outside the shop. Note that at this later date from the first photograph of the shop, that Fred has put out his advertisement below the shop window, 'Originators of the Jack Knife position'.

Figure 12 Joan Pratt and her friend Evelyn Hamilton a short time after the shop was opened.

Figure 11 Joan and Fred outside their new shop, note the tandem in the window display.

The shop

more about which later. This photograph was probably taken in late 1948 or early in 1949.

The business was doubtless formed in the mould that Fred had seen at CBs and he was quick to recruit a small staff to repair and to build his bicycles. In the early days whilst heading up the firm and training the staff, Fred would have been busy re-visiting old skills like wheel building that he had not had to use himself for nearly twenty years.

Time now to introduce to readers the second man in this story. Young Noel, the oldest of the growing Pratt family, grew up fast in the period before the war. Noel recalls the war period as a time of real privation. Then shortly after the war, cycling resumed for every one and by this time Noel had become keen on the sport, and was encouraged by his uncle, Reg Westgarth to take it up competitively.

Noel's Uncle Reg was also part of the Butler clan, being the husband of Claud's elder sister, Joyce. Reg was himself no mean cyclist and had been a real performer in his time. Noel joined the Kingston Phoenix Road Club (KPRC). Noel recalls that his first 25 race was a KPRC event on the Portsmouth Road. He remembers how indignant he was that "the rotters had put Reg one minute in front of me." When Noel went by after about three miles he heard the muffled 'Christ' and remembers that ever after it was a point of debate between them. Noel's time in that event, which had also been on his father's birthday, saw him beat his father's best time for that course. Noel could always thereafter face down Fred with that result when opinions differed in the shop.

Noel first went to work at age 14, just after the war, at Shannon Systems, an Office Equipment manufacturer. However, he left that employment to join the family enterprise when, two years later in 1948, the move to the shop happened. He notes, wryly, that as a family member of the firm, "my life was not encumbered by a wage packet, free labour by the family being a widely known fact. It was only when I started courting my future wife that I started to get 10s (now 50p) per week."

Figure 13 shows a young Noel probably somewhere on the A3 Portsmouth road in the 1940's.

Now for customers! Salfords is roughly halfway from the older town of Redhill and the then expanding new town of Crawley. Initially there would have been only a few interested local passers-by. We have the recollection of one, from Pat Illing, who is now a sprightly 70 odd year old. Pat lived in the small town of Horley four miles south had at the time just started at Reigate Grammar School and cycled passed the new shop twice a day. Pat was, he believes, the first customer in the shop but with the largesse of a schoolboy of the time he remembers that all he could afford to buy were some chromed set bolts for a Williams C34 chainset. He was impressed – or at least well remembers! - that the inside display surfaces of the shop were taken up with the Frederick Pratt cycling leaflets – of which more later.

Frederick knew that in addition to such casual trade he would need to capture regular trade from committed cyclists. This would for example be from members of the Redhill Cycle Club which had only recently been formed (in 1945) and which would become regularly supported by Fred and the family. Additionally, there was the Southern Wheelers, (since 1963 known as the Crawley Wheelers), who were based just six miles down the A23 around the new town of Crawley. These clubs needed to be wooed. Fred was still a keen CTC member and supporter and of course there would also be CTC members to be found. It was not long before the front of the shop was adorned by advertising well known to many cyclists - the attractive CTC winged wheel emblem and the National Clarion official Repairer's sign.

Fred and the shop

Many people have remarked on the warm welcome in the shop, where Joan was also able to hold forth. She did this whilst keeping the tea flowing on race days, and how she must have enjoyed being able to meet and see so many young and friendly faces and keep in contact with South London's, and the growing local, cycling club world. Fred was powerfully built and was probably addressed as Mr Pratt by most customers. Any casual customer who did not already know him, and who had gone in innocently enough for a small item was likely to have been stopped in their tracks. Given a chance, and Fred only needed a quarter of that, Fred would probably have lectured his new customer on the poor design that had led to the need for replacement of the part - from which he (Fred) was just about to profit. And then he might well have begun to tell them of his theories, if that is, they had not already gained some inkling that this was a man with a message from the numbers of his leaflets dotted round the cosy shop! More knowledgeable cyclists probably went in to enjoy, and egg on, Frederick's sermons on pedaling action and bicycle design. The little service road in front of the shop would have been congested with bicycles on Sundays and Public Holidays, as shown in Figure 14 which was taken in the 1950's. Just 3 or 4 shops along the little parade was the Gala tea-shop/cafe that became the unofficial Redhill Cycling Club headquarters.

Fred was obviously loved as a character. One of this well known, though non cycling activities kept a wide audience in gossip – at least to judge by the frequency the tale is retold! Every day almost without fail and certainly right round the year, Fred would be up early each morning for a swim in Earlswood Lakes, a local park. In Figure 15 Fred can be seen getting ready to swim with ice covering the lake's surface in 1959.

Figure 15 Fred prepares for an ice breaking swim.

Figure 14 Redhill Cycling Club Sunday morning ride in Salfords, 1950's

Fred and the shop

Figure 16 shows Fred, with Joan in attendance, after his icy bathe. One suspects however that this swim must have been a special event though to attract Joan out with him at this time and weather! In the summer he would often take Joan in the car and it would set them up for the day, with a return to the shop for about 1000. The lads in the shop, who had to start work at 0800, sometimes groaned at this indulgence! This swimming habit was a continuation of a practice he had indulged in before the war when on his way home from work he had swum in lakes near his route.

The shop would of course be open early on Sundays and race days. In those days the RTTC used the A23 between Earlswood and Crawley as part of a main drag course. The enthusiasm always showed in Joan's face, as she remembered details of those race days in the early 1950's. How, with the shop just a little way from a good long downhill section, she and Fred would stand in the shop door listening to the approach of the riders in the early morning mists. "You could always tell the fast men you know, that high pitched whine from their silk tubs was so much more exciting than the lower pitch hum from the cotton tubs used by the slower men!" Those, of course, were the days before the motor vehicle became king of the road, and when ambient noise levels were low. And after the race had gone through their shop would have been full of joking and occasionally buying friends, new and old, who as the throng thinned would stay on to wind up Fred and wait until mugs of tea were produced by Joan. Of course the first Sunday in November always saw the London to Brighton Veteran car event and the shop was an ideal and warm place from which to gather and chat away the morning.

The firm and its direction

Fred's original plans for the shop and the scope of the business have never been recorded. Perhaps it is possible to glean an insight into his intentions from the firm's brochures and the advertisements that he placed in the NCU Yearbooks[3] and occasionally in Cycling. These national advertisements seem to have been for bicycle repair and maintenance, rather than bicycle sales or the sale of an in house frame[4],

Figure 16 showing Fred and Joan after an icy dip for Fred in Earlswood lakes.

although in the later club publications his frames are highlighted. With the benefit of hindsight, and the experience of the decline in club cycling of the 1960's and 1970's in mind, Noel also feels that his father may have set up in too grand a fashion. He might have been better advised to develop the firm more slowly with just himself and perhaps one other. But who knows what was on Fred's mind? He may well have had financial targets to meet that, drawing his financial projections from experience with CB, indicated he had to go big, or at least of a certain size, in order to make the revenue needed.

Writing the history of a bicycle firm based on its advertising material is not ideal though it has often had to be used. It is frequently the only way in circumstances where the only records left by the chief protagonist or designer of a line, apart from the bikes themselves, are the firm's publications. Such a history can give an indication of what he or the firm was attempting to do or produce, though it can give a somewhat fixed-in-time, and therefore, a possibly only partially correct view.

The story that unfolds in the next section follows a short series of leaflets[5] which Fred himself prepared. If restricted to this base, it could not be the whole story of the Frederick bicycles —as the bicycles made by FHP&Son were named- rather this first story from the written work of Frederick Pratt covers only the history of one model, the Jack Knife, about which Fred himself wrote. There are no contemporary published accounts of the later more popular and more orthodox Frederick frames. This account of these beautifully made Fredericks is based largely on information from the frames and stories from their owners. These later frames are described in the section following that of the Jack Knife as they represent Fred's mellowing and acceptance of what his customers wanted. Noel and Pete Tester have given access to the firm's impromptu sales and build cards. Despite what may seem uncharacteristic reticence by Fred on these later frames, it is clear from his advertisements that he took great pride in the quality of the firm's work, and it is in fact these later bikes by which the bikes badged as Fredericks can be judged.

The Jack Knife

A number of older cyclists remember the Frederick name for just one particular reason, the short lived Jack Knife model, or as it is known to Noel, and as the family called it, the trailer bike. The trailer bike was borne from the ideas for cycling efficiency and good bike design developed by Frederick Pratt and promoted by him to what appears to have been a sceptical, sometimes raucously amused, audience. The story given here is Fred's own account, taken from the four leaflets that the firm issued. The leaflets were never dated, but Noel recalls them as having been written before the shop was opened. The reference to Noel's involvement in the Jack Knife's evolution in Leaflet Four indicates that at least this last one must have written about 1948. They were most probably issued in 1949, but it is conceivable that numbers 1 to 2 could have been available from the opening of the shop in 1948.

The story in the four leaflets is the theory, researched, agonized over, and written up by Fred probably in the run up to his leaving CBs, probably whilst looking for his new premises and dreaming about opening his own new business. The historic sequence is largely as described in the fourth and last of the leaflets. It was here that Fred felt the need to describe the origin of his ideas for the Jack Knife frame.

As already noted, Fred had built track machines for the 1936 six day races. Noel recalls Fred recounting how seeing some of the strongest riders becoming tired very easily. Their tiredness and strain, was induced, he felt, by poor frame design (the overly steep angles). This convinced him that these features were limiting optimal performance. Fred had himself built the frames in question, though only under duress, as the riders had insisted upon having a 75 head and seat tube angle, a 1 inch front fork rake, and very little clearance from seat tube to rear wheel. One particularly strong rider virtually collapsed near the end of the race. The conclusion drawn by Fred was that this current racing frame design was too extreme in its angles and the bikes had become almost un-ridable.

Fred considered that this prevalent design tendency gave a stance on a bicycle that was too upright. He was always happy to recall how bikes that he had built for the Belgian national six day team, using his frame design, with relaxed frame angles, had been scorned when first shown to the riders. However, after the team had won the event on them, they changed their views and afterwards complimented Fred on the design. He knew he was right, and indeed, contemporary articles in the cycling press, show he was not alone[6]. Nevertheless, he knew how difficult it would be to fly in the face of fashion and the 'established' rules of frame design. Figure 17 shows the solution.

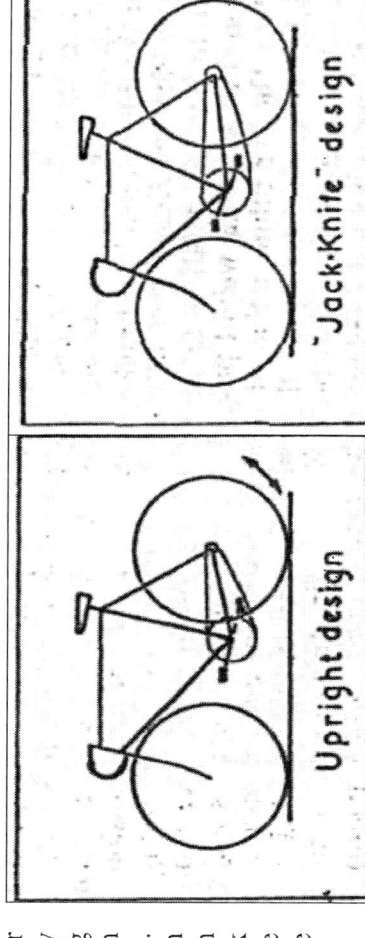

Figure 17 Fred's diagrams of his two opposing frame cases

Fred needed to prove his theories, and as Chief Engineer to CBs he needed a rational well thought out approach. Later, these thoughts were shared by Cycling's own design guru, though how deep this support was within the bicycle buying world is rather debatable.[7]

Fred described, in the last leaflet, how in 1940 he had built himself a frame for road use. This bike can be seen in Figure 18 which shows Noel Pratt riding it after the war.

The bike had features resembling Fred's own first racing bike of the early 1920's with relaxed head and seat tube angles about 68° and 65° respectively, and Fred also gave it a long wheel-base using a extra long rear triangle of 26 inches. This frame was thus in opposition to the then current sports / racing bike "upright design."

Figure 18 Noel riding the Trailer bike - see space between rear wheel and the seat tube mounted pump and note the special rack built by Fred.

The Jack Knife

The name Trailer bike given to Fred's brain child with the family was that, when riding it, it initially felt as though one was towing a trailer. A little incidental evidence of how closely the Pratt family lived and worked together may perhaps be seen here by another pencil sketch from Joan's album. This is shown in Figure 19.

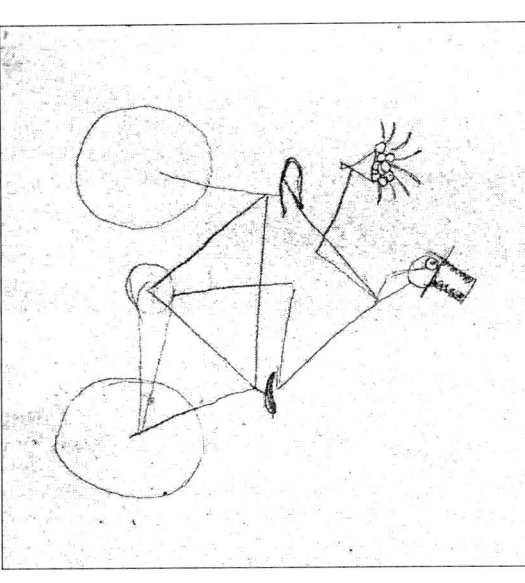

Figure 19 A casual sketch or doodling by Joan Pratt

Scant evidence perhaps if what you see is just a doodle. But, to the more partial eye, the simple line drawing, with its exaggeratedly long rear triangle, can be none other than Fred's new design, drawn accurately, though perhaps not to a draughtman's standard!, by his adoring wife.

Fred found his new frame to be comfortable and relaxing once the requisite leg muscles had become attuned to it. This frame was regularly used by Fred and he built up a special lightweight rear carrier in position. In the leaflet Fred notes, "This machine caused much amusement and criticism and suffered many belittling remarks, but my mind was made up and I would not be deterred." Fred's strong principles, later to be so valued and enjoyed by his shop customers, were beginning to be formulated!

The story in the leaflet continued by explaining how Noel acted as the unpaid chief tester of the frame. Since the age of 10, and as he grew into full bike size, Noel was riding bikes made especially for him with Fred's preferred 'relaxed' angles. Noel rode these bikes enthusiastically as a schoolboy, although he does now admit that one reason that he found bike riding particularly attractive was that he could avoid becoming involved with helping his father on a landscaping binge. He found the bike a good escape! Shortly after the war Fred built a new experimental bike with similar angles to the others he had built for Noel but with a shorter top-tube length and slightly greater rear triangle length. The inevitable toe overlap on this machine worried Joan but Noel was allowed to use it, after reassuring his mother he could cope. He loved it and was given a pair of wooden sprints for it at Christmas 1947. This is probably the bicycle seen in Figure 20.

Figure 20 Noel riding the pre-production Jack Knife

It was whilst this frame was away being professionally stove enameled that Noel "inherited" the old original trailer bike to use in the interim. Noel immediately felt that this bike, was, as it were, the real Jack Knife, and was the better of the two. Noel used this bicycle for a number of very promising time trials, and both he and his father thought there was considerable promise in the design. It was also used in grass track events by Noel who obviously loved it. Unfortunately the historical account of the Jack Knife in Leaflet 4 finishes at this point, which seems to confirm that this last leaflet was written before opening the shop stopped such research. This would therefore have been in 1948.

Fred's account of the background to the Jack Knife shows that there must have been at least three early prototype Jack Knife frames and it seems likely that Fred would have wanted some of his own frames on sale in the shop when he could. Fred acknowledged that the Jack Knife design was too extreme and states that all the Jack Knife bikes sold were the less unorthodox style known in the shop as Jack

The Jack Knife

Knife Applied. The earliest production frame that is presently known about is No 4911. This frame which appears to have been a Jack Knife Applied was owned from new by Pat Illing, whom was first mentioned in this account as a young schoolboy entering the new shop. There is no contemporary published description of this frame in the cycling press. Pat reports that his did not ride well, so it was later modified to more orthodox angles and then went overseas with a family friend never to return. It seems quite likely from its frame number and Noel's account of the development of the Frederick that it may be only the fourth Frederick frame as it must have been built early in the year, and could have been the first frame to have been built in January 1949, just a few months after the shop was opened.

Why the name Jack Knife? Perhaps to understand that as Fred intended we need to go back to the other leaflets, Numbers 1, 2 and 3 all of which are reprinted with this account.

In the first leaflet, which was entitled "The Jack Knife Position", Fred set out the ideal bicycle shape and justified it. His argument was that less steep angles and good resilient forks with adequate fork offset allowed the rider to relax and, as these angles were reduced, so any skittishness by the bike was also reduced. The term "Jack Knife" came from his thesis that the ideal position of the rider's body would have the angle between the arms and the legs kept to a reasonable minimum to ensure maximum muscular efficiency (arms in tension, legs in compression). The human body shape was thus likened to that of a partially open jack knife, and the action of using a Jack Knife frame as akin to closing such a knife. The sub-title of Leaflet 1 says it all "it closes the angle as closing the Jack Knife." The virtue of the Jack Knife frame seen by Fred was that a short top-tube and the straight-line of arm to front axle gave sensitive and direct steering feel. At the same time responsive front forks with a relative large fork offset helped keep the front wheel on the ground and not weaving about due to bumping. It also meant that pedaling action caused less pendulum effect on the bottom bracket as this was nearer the stiff front of the frame and further away from the rear wheel than on bikes with the "Upright position." This latter meant there was less disturbance of the rear wheel which in turn allowed the vital forwarding propulsion forces between road and the rear tyre to be more stable. In contrast, according to Fred, with steep angled frames, the rear wheel would hop around the road due to excessive bottom bracket twitches (known in Fred's terms, as sidewards wag) which were caused by a short and stiff rear triangle. Fred also noted that on a steep angled bike the cyclist's head would be in a looking down stance, and the neck have to be strained upwards in order to look forward. However, by providing more 'relaxed' frame angles and tilting the body backwards, as in the Jack Knife position, the head could be kept more upright. This obviously gave a safer pose for road awareness when riding.

Conscious of the difficulty that some riders had with toe overlap, Fred ended the comments on the Jack Knife in this first leaflet with an admonition not to steer the bike by turning the bars, but by leaning the bike. He saw this leaning action as a part of "Riding the front wheel" and as being easier on a Jack Knife frame with its emphasis on putting the rider closer to the front wheel. On the last page of this first part of his polemic Fred set out the opposite position to that which he advised – one which he felt was thoroughly wrong - and ended with words which say as much as :- 'Watch the rear wheel of the sprinters and see if you cannot see the twitching and skittishness that indicates the error of their ways!'

In the second leaflet Fred expounded on good pedaling – "Pedaling with a purpose" – and set out by means of a series of diagrams the advantages of achieving a smooth circular action. This action he called the cat's claw action. This is fully described in the original in Appendix D but is also shown in Figure 21 for readers' convenience.

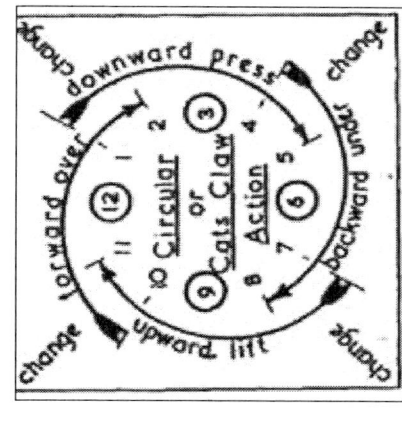

Figure 21 The Cat's claw Action

Fred considered that this pedaling action should have four phases – Downward Press, then the Backward Under, the Upward Lift and finally the Forward Over. In his view, this action was the most efficient action, to be replaced only on hills or in acceleration by the Thrusting Action where the foot's action was more that of the piston of an internal combustion engine on the power stroke. Fred merely remarks in this leaflet that the cat's claw motion can be combined with the Jack Knife frame for effective and efficient cycling.

In the third leaflet Fred sets out what he considers the poor design points of the "Upright position", and contrasts these with the advantages of the Jack Knife as identified above. This leaflet is perhaps more critical of the rest of the cycling world's design aims than the first two in the series.

Fred mentions in Leaflet 4, which is in a sense his "magnum opus", the strong disagreements of others to his design. This may be why, in that last leaflet, he justified his design simply by explaining how he got the ideas, instead of trying to present his case by using engineering logic. Could it be that his strong refutations of the existing design tendency to use upright angles made in the third leaflet, had already polarised a sceptical cycling world against the Jack Knife? It does seem likely that the Jack Knife design met with considerable customer resistance, at least from those who were already wedded to orthodoxy.

The Jack Knife

At this point, it is perhaps appropriate to introduce another fascinating period feature piece.

This is Fred's epic poem.

Once a lad with time on hand
Desired to travel o'er the land.
First he tarried on a hike,
Then his thoughts turned to a bike.
Sleep head, long reach, all continental,
Bright paint and gadgets ornamental.
He rode well but had to rest,
The handlebars were never best,
Pedal place not just so,
Best attempts were always slow.
Anxious to improve condition
He tried a bike JACK KNIFE position.
He first attempted with a thrill
The THRUSTING ACTION up a hill,
Over the top with great success
From UPWARD LIFT to DOWN PRESS
A scrapping crowd was next attention
He passed them all with CATS CLAW ACTION.

By Frederick H Pratt

There appears to be no recorded history of the Jack Knife frame beyond the point mentioned in Leaflet 4 where Noel's initial good performances were thought to be encouraging indications for the design. The completion of Leaflet 4 containing the Jack Knife write up was probably late 1948 with, as already noted, the first three leaflets written earlier. Any later and it is likely that Fred's time would have been taken up by developing his new firm. Thus during 1949 he would have been busy as he had to take on and train up Pete Tester to replace his first frame building assistant, the more experienced Derek Pullen, who left the firm when it was still struggling to find its customer base. Also at this time Fred and Noel's attention to cycling was disrupted by Noel's two-year break for National Service, finally starting in December 1950. Noel's joining the Army was delayed on commercial grounds for six months. Fred was obviously able to make a good case to the Army recruiting office that Noel was critical for the young and struggling firm. By the time Noel was back in Salfords in December 1952, the time of the Jack Knife appears to have been almost over – see discussion later on.

Purpose of the leaflets

Why did Fred write the leaflets? Was Fred really concerned with just getting over his message about bike design and cycling efficiency to his customers, or was he hoping to build himself a good market with them and their end product the Jack Knife? Should we take the leaflets at face value as just Fred setting down some of the truths that he had distilled from his years at CBs? Each leaflet has the following by-line above the individual title line – "We learn by Teaching". Perhaps Fred had added that after he had spent many an hour in the saddle and in evenings at home mulling over what he should be telling fellow cyclists.

Noel is dismissive of the idea that the leaflets and their extension in metal, the Jack Knife frame design, were just a ploy by Fred to help spread the name of his new firm. He is emphatic that the answer to that suggestion is "No!" Nevertheless, the discussions that any unique frame would have started amongst avid cycling 'techies' over frame design, together with the sight of Noel competing on the end product – a fast Jack Knife machine - would have made good publicity for the fledgling firm. See the young man flying on the 1947 pre-production bike already shown in Figure 20. After all, major companies such as Baines, Bates, Leach, Moorson, Rensch (Paris), Saxon and Sun all had at one time or another had easily recognised models with unique frame geometry so that their products could readily be identified in magazine photographs of fastmen winning races - and who is to say that any of these famous designs gave any significant mechanical advantage?

Fred would also have recognised just how much his old firm CBs used publicity to good effect in increasing awareness of their brand, hence aiding sales. CB's advertisements and his lavish brochures used strong declarations of his scientific approach to designs, and to lugless construction. Fred, of course on his smaller budget, and simpler life style, could not have afforded or indeed wanted to emulate the later Claud tricks such as encouraging a CB owning community to meet at CBs evening entertainments- the "Claud Do's".[8] But it seems very likely he saw his leaflets as creating useful publicity – and then of course he had a small trick – he charged for them. Quite modest pricing – the first three were 4d each or 10d for all three to be posted, and Number 4, which gave away his Jack Knife frame's secrets, was definitely a resounding bargain at 6d.

What do other people think about Fred's views? Mike Burrows was asked to review the four leaflets for this account. He telephoned several days later. "I've been reading these with great interest", he said, then "Who was Frederick Pratt? Was he some sort of gifted amateur – a kind of artisan philosopher?" Well, perhaps that is gilding Mike's comments just a little!

In reviewing Mike's comments it is as well to recall that he occupies an eminent position in the design of both competition and everyday bicycles, some 50 years on from Fred's time. Mike is of course acclaimed as designer to World Record holders and to the largest cycle manufacturer in the world. He can view bicycle design from a pinnacle of scientifically derived design studies – indeed, relatively speaking, from a mountain plateau of systematic study and knowledge – which was simply not available when Fred Pratt was developing his ideas.

Mike's view on Fred's pedaling advice (Leaflet 2) was, that yes, it was a plausible system; and in terms of the advice to obtain a smooth rotational movement (Fred's CIRCULAR ACTION) it was wholly acceptable. Indeed he commented, until the last decade or so it was a system he could have accepted as genuine good advice. Where he now felt he had to differ, was that modern sports physiology research has recently shown that trying to use the follow-through foot to lift the returning pedal leads to excessive work for the foot muscles. If the prime aim of the competitive cyclist is maximum power, it is not helpful. Basically there is only so much oxygen that can reach the foot and leg muscles in time when cycling hard. The research shows that pushing down with the foot and leg for about one sixth of a rotation (when the rotations per minute are 90 to 100) is about as much as most people can manage. Above this rate, or if the muscles of the foot are trying to do more per revolution, the muscles become starved of oxygen and are also unable to get rid of lactic acid, which is the by-product of muscle work. Better to perfect your smooth action with a simple down-stroke. In Fred's defense, it should be noted that he had recognized that in racing action, and when accelerating, the more piston like Thrusting Action would be needed.

Fred's views on the usefulness of "pulling strongly on the bars using the arms" (Jack Knife position, Leaflet 1) were dismissed by Mike as not true. He did allow, however, that on hills and in sprints the arms could significantly assist in the action. He also noted that, from research on recumbent riding – and again there is no one better qualified to comment than Mike - there could be something to be said for it. The argument is that when the legs are the sole muscle group in action, the circulation can struggle to provide adequate blood supply to satisfy the demand from the leg muscles, and cannot disperse lactic acid rapidly enough. In this condition it somehow helps that the arm and chest muscles are now included in the demand. This is probably because the wider blood circulation through the body allows a more general dispersion and dilution of lactic acid in the blood stream. So may be, on this one too, Fred had some thing there.

Purpose of the leaflets

Turning to frame angles, Mike is clearly in his own area of direct research and experience. He noted that, in terms of head angles, his own work reported in his book Bicycle Design[9] revealed that changing head angles between say 69 and 76 gave so little difference in handling that the differences were "mostly in the rider's head". He also noted that the experienced rider could usually detect the changes and the degree of feedback. However from his own personal experiences he has stated in Bicycle Design that "as long as the rider detects and understands this change in the bike's response, he can ride road race, velodrome, or probably even off road, on the same head angle."

Dealing with weight distribution over the wheels and the long wheelbase, Mike is dismissive of the need to be prescriptive over cycle design. He regards both these attributes as personal preference and, quoting recumbent racing as showing a wide range of machines which can have an equally wide variation in weight distribution and wheel base, comments in Bicycle Design- "Any difference in cornering speed you will quickly realise is due to rider rather than machine."

In terms of the position of the rider's weight being in front rather than behind the bottom bracket, Mike feels Fred was just plain wrong. However, Mike didn't want to end his review on a negative note, because as much as many a cyclist, and perhaps more than most, he loves to discuss bike design and certainly wouldn't want to stifle it. He notes that there is no doubt that a long wheelbase does give an indefinably comfortable and positive feel to a bike; a view probably shared by many a roadster rider.

He ended with the thought that one of his own latest bikes, the box carrier bike known as Freight-Eight, was a long wheelbase machine and he is just loving riding it. Were there any problems, he mused? ôMay be a bit of wheel spin is possible when starting off". Well, there are two observations on that comment. The first is that such wheel spin has to be an attribute that would endear such a bike to any cyclist, especially if, uncritically or small boy like, he thought that it was the bike that enabled him to achieve that macho wheel spin. Perhaps that was Fred's finding too! The second point on wheel spin is that it could be this is the feature or at least a contributory effect to it, which has been reported by several other owners, that the Jack Knife was not so good when hill climbing. See Clive Oxx's comments at the end of this story.

Pat Illing is the only other known rider of a Jack Knife or Jack Knife style frame. Pat owned several relaxed angle bikes in the Jack Knife mode. We have already covered the fact that that his 4911 (probably originally a Jack Knife Applied design) was returned to the shop for modification by Pat. Pat reports that whilst these changes were made, Fred lent him the early prototype with a 46 inch wheel base, 1 inch down tube and a very short bottom bracket to front wheel distance. This gave an almost dangerous toe clip overlap, but "you got used to that even with a fixed. It was an extremely rigid and steady machine but curiously unresponsive despite its rigidity." The chain length was enormous and Pat found the long chain stays allowed a lot of chain slap, though he did note some of this could have been caused by the lack of concentricity that was common in Williams chainwheels of the time.

What other early 1950's riders thought about the Jack Knife frame, and about Fred's written cycling dogmas in the Leaflets, has not been recorded in contemporary cycling publications. Thus it is difficult to explain the failure of the design to take-off commercially, other than the sheer difference the machine showed to its contemporary competitors. Towards the end of this account are some snippets about an apparently similar and now retro design in the 1990's – and then the contemporary commentators were indeed vocal!

The later frames

The only known records to survive after Joan burnt the shop's records following Fred's death are some rough notes for frames to be built for specific customers' orders. These were scribbled points for each frame taken by Noel or Pete when the order was made. A transcription of these notes, the originals of which are written on all sorts of scraps of paper or card packaging, such as the inside of inner tube boxes and such like, has been set out in Appendix B. There is also a records which had been started as a consecutive listing from 1951 to the last frame built in 1967. This had been set down in Noel's workshop diary, which was a 1949 Electrical Engineers diary. Noel was away in the National Service from December 1950 to December 1952. He was therefore not in the country at the date of the first of these records, in February 1951, which must therefore have been made by Fred or Pete Tester somewhere else and then copied into the diary on Noel's return. Pete Tester's building technique, learnt from Fred who built the first couple of frames with him, to a month later when a gleaming new frame was back from the painting firm. It was to hand-saw the mitres using, as his eye became more expert, just two cuts per mitre, and attempting to get a perfect fit with the minimum of filing. The start was to locate the top tube and head, then set out the frame using a 'unique-to-the-customer' paper drawing which was taped to a sheet of plate glass. The frame's main triangle was laid out, then brazed up, after the key joints had been pegged with framing pins. Pete recalled the lugs were usually Haden with the imported Nervex lugs used on the best frames and later the plainer Prugnat type, though early machines used anything available, cf frame 4971 which was built with two righthand rear dropouts! FHP&Son were often able to obtain scarce building materials through CBs that other small builders had to do without.

All frames were made in Reynolds double butted 531 except where unusual tube strength was needed. In the early days it was normal for a batch of frames to be made and then taken to be sand blasted in South London by a specialist. They then passed the frames on to be stove enameled by CBs, who were known at that time for the quality of their frame enameling. Later, after the CB factory closed, another small enameller, James Gray in Tooting, took on the work. Later again, James Gray closed and the frames then went to Holdsworth for all finishing work. The firm found that the previously friendly and cosy relationship, enjoyed with CBs and James Gray, was replaced by what the firm felt was a mean spirited "business only" relationship with Holdsworth. This was much resented by the erstwhile family members at Salfords, and the tales of Holdsworth meanness were the stuff of legends.

In the early days the shop tended to fit to a customer's frame whatever accessories the trade supplied. Later, and if the buyers were well-off, they might have been able to have what they had read about in the cycling journals of the time. The shop would normally fit trade components (from un-identified makers). What is now, some 50 years later, thought of as very ordinary lightweight gear - Williams C34 or may be C1000 and Phillips or GB brakes, was in itself an expensive indulgence for most buyers. In this area of club-land the continental exotica was to all intents and purposes unobtainable for young men on normal salaries.

Noel has told me that the frame numbering system was an annual series, based upon Y/m/x where, in 581113, Y is year 1958 =58, m is month November =11, and x is the consecutive frame number within the year = 13 in this case. This system was maintained for the first ten years from 1951 to 1960, but thereafter the system was simplified to Y/x with the month omitted. The month shown is the month when the shop completed the frame; the order would have been finally completed a few weeks to a month later when a gleaming new frame was back from the painting firm. It was not unknown for keen racers to collect bare frames from the shop and use them unpainted to get the new bike ready for the new season.

Due to this numbering system – one that is not fully consecutive between years - it is not possible to know the total number of frames made. Similarly, because the surviving records start in 1951, how many earlier frames had been made, or indeed if frames were made but not for some reason given a FHP & Son number, is not known. So there may well be quite a few more that remain unrecorded. For example, Pat Illing bought a second-hand Frederick from the shop in the 1990's which is stamped number 5959. This number does not appear in Noel's listings. Interestingly there were some frames that were built earlier than 1951. These frames may have had numbers (as in the case of 4911 which was also owned by Pat Illing and which has already been mentioned) but their records have not been found and which possibly amongst those burnt by Joan.

The number of frames listed in the available records is 205. Noel is clear that the last frame was made in 1967. So, allowing for perhaps another twenty or so frames made before the shop was opened or when Noel was overseas, a probable production of 225 frames, or 250 at the outside, seems likely for the twenty odd years 1948 to 1967. This number agrees with Noel's and Pete's recollections.

Most of the records kept in the shop show frame numbers and sizes with occasionally the frame colours ordered by the customers, but give no other details except in rare cases such as the two tandems and lugless frames. There was at least one Jack Knife tandem, which may have been the frame No 5266. 5214 is known to have been a one off custom frame made for Pat Illing by Pete Tester to Pat's own design. This

The later frames

was lugless with relaxed angles (68/67), a top-tube of 1? inch diameter and a down tube of 1 diameter and is shown in Figures 22 to 24.

Figure 22 Frame 5214 showing oversize top tube and relaxed head and seat angles

Figure 23 Frame 5214 showing lugless head and early head transfer

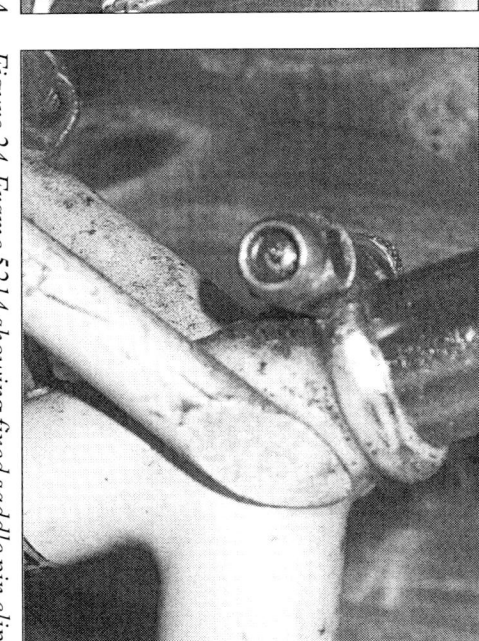

Figure 24 Frame 5214 showing fixed saddle pin clip

Although this unique custom frame was made specifically to the owner's requirements, the slack angles are perhaps the last evidence of Jack Knife influence in the shop? Thought perhaps you could argue they are just a figment of their time. In Appendix B frame and fittings data for 1961 to 1960 are provided as an illustration – and a record for posterity – of the details of a minor frame builder in this period. These workshop records are available courtesy of Noel Pratt and Colin Heath; they had been previously mislaid and then forgotten, being found only when the shop was being finally being cleared.

The more complete series records are listed in Appendix A, and the comments which follow are largely inferences from this simple record of frame purchasers/orders and their frame numbers. The first question was "When was the Frederick frame

at its most popular?" This appears, as seen in Figure 25, to be the late 1950's and early '60's.

There are three periods, each one leading to a peak, which can be seen in the graph of the records shown as Figure 25. Assuming that the shop and the popularity of its frames was due to the availability of good attractive frames at a fair price, the following could be argued. The most obvious reason for these three peaks in production would be that they were simply periods when Redhill Cycling Club was particularly active. Of course, it could also be that these periods could just be three periods when two or more builders were busy at the hearth at the same time! If this was the case the first period, in the early 1950's, could have been when the firm was becoming established with Pete Tester getting established and Noel back from National Service. The second period might be explained as being when the enthusiastic Richard Woods joined the shop, but then this period was also a time of general prosperity, as in MacMillan's 1958 - "You've never had it so good." - speech. The third and last period in 1966 is not so easy to explain. It might be just an artificial bleep that 12 frames were built, not for specific customers as was usually the case, but all for stock. However, this period was when Fred was terminally ill and the cycle trade at one of its lowest points. It would not be surprising if the staff had just got on with frame building to support the firm in the hope that if they kept their heads down all would come right. Unfortunately, it did not; Fred died in 1967 and the firm had to lose all but the family members in order to survive.

The later frames

Month	1951	1952	1953	1954	1955	1956	1957	1958	1959	1960	Total 1951-60	Mthly mean 1951-60	Mthly median 1951-60
Jan	-	1	2	5	1	1	-	6	3	1	20	2	1
Feb	1	2	1	2	-	1	-	1	-	4	12	1	1
Mar	1	-	2	4	2	1	1	-	3	2	16	2	1
Apr	2	1	4	2	-	-	1	1	3	-	13	1	1
May	1	-	-	1	-	2	2	1	-	1	8	1	1
Jun	1	2	2	-	-	-	1	1	2	-	9	1	1
Jul	-	-	-	-	-	-	-	-	1	3	5	1	-
Aug	1	-	-	1	-	-	2-	1	1	5	8	1	1
Sep	-	1	-	-	-	-	-	-	3	-	7	1	-
Oct	-	2	-	1	-	-	-	1	-	2	7	1	-
Nov	1	1	-	-	1	-	-	3	3	2	10	1	1
Dec	1	2	1	-	-	-	-	2	3	-	9	1	-
Year	9	12	12	17	4	5	6	17	22	20	124	12 annual	12 annual

Table 1 Monthly records of Frederick frames for the ten years 1951 to 1960

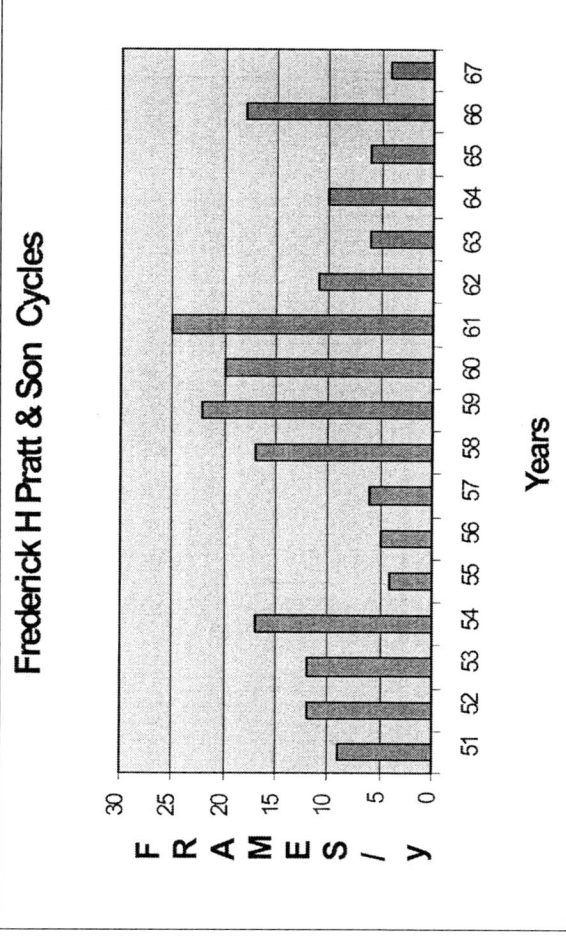

Figure 25 Annual frame building numbers from 1951 to 1967

Seasonal variations in production throughout the year can be seen by making use of the month of completion (given in the frame number). This monthly analysis is shown in Table 1 overleaf. It has only been possible to carry out the analysis for the first ten years of Noel's record as after that for some now unknown reason the frame numbering system was simplified and from then on only yearly totals are available.

The analysis shows that on average 12 frames were built each year and that most were ordered in the first three months of the year, presumably for the new competition year. One possibly revealing statistic is the median value, (the value exceeded for 50 percent of the time) for each month of the year. This value is shown in the column on the extreme right of Table 1. These values support what is already known, that just one frame would be sold per month but this would typically only be in the first five months of the year. Of course the shop would have been much busier with casual work in the summer months and might not have been able to make frames due to work with repairs from both racing men and the whole range of non racing cyclists. It is probable that some of the leisure riders would only get their bikes out during the summer, and might hardly have used the shop at other times of year.

It is interesting to look now at the owners of the frames, as listed by Noel and seen in Table A1 (in Appendix A in this account). To put the fair sex first, it is intriguing to see only six orders (out of 200 odd) by or for ladies in the list. One of them was for Olive Wyles, who was RCC's Lady Champion in the late 1940's. Indeed the RCC are the majority group amongst the owners in the list. Peter Crowsley, who was racing at this time, noted that "one seldom saw a Jack Knife about, except when racing on the Cherry Tree course, (the RTTC G9 which went through Salfords and which was also a RCC home course), there, it seemed they were all on them!" Though it seems, in retrospect, from the findings of these researches that Peter's recollection of the number of Jack Knife bikes may be suffering from golden boyhood memories?

Table 2 on the next page shows the names of people who supported the firm by buying over the years more than one frame. Many were RCC racing men replacing their bikes each year for one or two years then possibly leaving the sport, others started that way, cooled, and then came back 10 years or so later to buy another frame, perhaps for touring. And the key 'owner', the man who beat the wheel at Monte Carlo? – well, of course, that was Pete Tester, frame builder extra-ordinaire, and no mean racer, who doubtless used the frames to carry the FHP & S flag – or in this case the shop window - to club life. And equally likely Fred, who was known to be overly generous when Joan wasn't looking, let some of those same frames go to new likely lads from RCC or elsewhere. And, it may be, that just one of those lads was Clive Oxx to whom Fred extolled the virtues of the Jack Knife back in 1952.

Thus the multiple owners listed in Table 2, and there were just eighteen of them, owned almost a quarter of the total Frederick production.

The later frames

Table 2 Multiple purchasers of frames

Year	1951	1952	1953	1954	1955	1956	1957	1958	1959	1960	1961	1962	1963	1964	1965	1966	1967	Total Number
Pete Tester	1	1	1	2	1	1	1	2	1									11
Pat Illing		1											1					5*
F Marshall	1	2																4
Gordon Ball	1	1		1							1							4
Noel Pratt			1						1			1						4
Ken Bean			1						1			1						3
Scott				2														2
J Poat							2											2
Bob Black								1			2							3
Ward									1		1							2
Fabb family									2									2
Smithers										1	1							2
Corsini										2								2
Burrell fam												1		1		1		3
Peter Head														1		1		2
J Pratt														1			1	2
O'Donnell															2			2
Hart family																1	1	2

* Pat Illing owns a 1949 *Jack Knife* (4911 RIP!) and also owns a 1959 frame (5959), neither of which were found in the records made by Noel Pratt

The existing records which are transcribed in Appendices A and B only cover the middle and later years, and do not identify many frame details, nor record the early frames. This is a shame because it would be fascinating to know how many frames of the Jack Knife style were made and sold.

However, there could be other clues about how long this model was for sale. The Jack Knife itself was never sold, only the Jack Knife Applied – the less extreme version of the idea– was supplied by the shop. There are however, some clues from a series of advertisements in the pocket sized Members Handbooks of the Redhill Cycle Club[10], which may indicate the run of the model. Figure 26 shows the advertisements from 1949 to 1952 and Figure 27 the later 1953 to 1957 range. There was no 1954 advertisement in the booklet as the Club had a lean patch and that year's handbook was typed rather than printed. Finally in Figure 28 is a later 1950's advertisement. This is from the Southern Wheeler's magazine Wheeler's News, kindly provided by Tony Killick.

The advertisements show that in 1949, with the shop having been open less than a year, the firm was advertising itself as the Originators of the Jack Knife position, arguably also referring to a bold new frame design. Incidentally this same slogan was used at this time on the shop front as was seen in Figure 12. Two years later the shop was described as the pioneer of the Jack Knife. Did being a pioneer imply there were others – and that there were copiers around? Were there any known con-

The later frames

1949

FREDERICK H. PRATT & SON
Complete Cycle Engineer

ORIGINATORS OF THE
Jack Knife Position

- Particulars of this Frederick Frame Sets by request.
- Illustrated Instructive leaflets Nos. 1, 2, 3, and 4, for 1/4d. P.O.

We LEARN by TEACHING!

Brighton Roads, Salfords, Surrey

1950

THIS IS A FREE COUNTRY...
you buy what you like where you like
BUT REMEMBER...
Fred Pratt and his staff are always ready to give preferential service to club folk

We are qualified and can deal with any job
We are experienced and can advise with wisdom on cycles and cycling.
We keep shop hours which lend to your convenience
We have good stocks and will quickly obtain special items
We want to do our best for you

SO...

If the bulge in your Maes bends
Or your Mafac Racer brakes
Bring them in, we weld things up
And put bent things back straight.
If your head feels tight or loose
Or you've a ball or two worn out
We can always put you right
Just you give us a shout!

FREDERICK H. PRATT & SON
BRIGHTON ROAD, SALFORDS.   HORLEY 1165

1951

FREDERICK H. PRATT & SON.
F.I.Cyc.T.
COMPLETE CYCLE ENGINEERS.
Pioneers of the
JACK KNIFE position

ALL ★ THIS FREDERICK
accessories ★ frame sets built to any
stocked   design from £12-15-0
Plain
agencies ★ COMPLETE MACHINES
held   to your own specification
(easy Terms)

EXPERT ADVICE FREELY GIVEN

BRIGHTON ROAD, SALFORDS, SURREY

1952

FREDERICK H. PRATT & SON.
F.I.Cyc.T.

GIVES A MONEY BACK GUARANTEE ON ALL REPAIR WORK, INCLUDING:—
WELDING, BRAZING, ENAMELLING, WHEELBUILDING, ETC.

With skill and interest we will take pleasure building your special frame.

From £10 15 0 Welded Construction
"   £13 13 0 Incorporating Lugs
For Cash or Convenient Easy Terms

ALL ACCESSORIES STOCKED
EXPERT ADVICE WITH PLEASURE
PREFERENTIAL TREATMENT EXTENDED TO ALL CLUB MEMBERS

BRIGHTON ROAD, SALFORDS.

Figure 26 Four years min-advertisements in the RCC Year book 1949-52.

1953

Frederick H. Pratt & Son
SPECIALISTS CYCLE BUILDERS AND REPAIRERS

We will make
Your Frame
under Our transfer

COMPLETE CYCLES, FRAMES, WHEELS, TUBULARS AND ALL ACCESSORIES supplied for cash or on easy terms
FROM **£2** DEPOSIT

Frame alterations and all repairs undertaken.

SATISFACTION or money refunded on all work done by us.

Brighton Road, Salfords, Surrey
Phone: HORLEY 1165

1955

FREDERICK H. PRATT & SON
MAKERS OF THE "FREDERICK"
HAND-BUILT FRAME

COMPLETE CYCLES, FRAMES, WHEELS TUBULARS, CLOTHING AND ALL PARTS supplied for cash or on easy terms
TERMS FROM **£1** DEPOSIT

FRAME ALTERATIONS & ALL REPAIRS UNDERTAKEN

SATISFACTION or money refunded on all work done by us.

Brighton Road, Salford, Surrey
Phone: HORLEY 1165

1956

FREDERICK H. PRATT & SON
Makers of the "FREDERICK"
HAND BUILT FRAME

COMPLETE CYCLES, FRAMES, WHEELS TUBULARS, CLOTHING & ALL PARTS supplied for cash or on easy terms
TERMS FROM **£1** DEPOSIT

FRAME ALTERATIONS & ALL REPAIRS UNDERTAKEN

SATISFACTION or money refunded on all work done by us.

Brighton Road, SALFORD, Surrey.
Phone: HORLEY 1165

1957

FREDERICK H. PRATT & SON
Makers of the "FREDERICK"
HAND BUILT FRAME

COMPLETE CYCLES, FRAMES, WHEELS TUBULARS, CLOTHING & ALL PARTS supplied for cash or on easy terms
TERMS FROM **£1** DEPOSIT

FRAME ALTERATIONS & ALL REPAIRS UNDERTAKEN

SATISFACTION or money refunded on all work done by us.

Brighton Road, Salford, Surrey.
Phone: HORLEY 1165

Figure 27 Another four years from the RCC Yearbooks

The later frames

temporary copies made by other builders? Or did the use of the word 'pioneer' imply they had started what became a standard? Whatever, from 1951 onwards the Redhill CC Handbook advertisements do not mention the Jack Knife model and instead only mention 'the Hand-built frame,' whilst the later advertisement as in Figure 28 seems to imply the virtue of the small custom maker approach.

In the first few years frames were sold at 12 guineas to 15 guineas for the frame and forks, but this had risen to 17 guineas and a little more at the close of frame building in 1967. In 1949 Fred had commissioned head and down-tube transfers. The original head transfer is shown in Figure 29. This design was often also used on the seat tube.

The down-tube script is shown in Figure 30. Noel recalls the upset that this down tube set of transfers caused. Fred had sent his draft of the design to the transfer maker who had used Fred's art work direct for the production transfers as he thought it was the final version. Ever the perfectionist, Fred was livid: but faced with a large num-

---

FREDERICK CYCLE FRAMES
are actually made on the premises of **Frederick Pratt & Son, 32 Brighton Rd, Salford,** Personally supervised and constructed by an enthusiastic staff, to your personal instructions.

WE ONLY MAKE CLASS JOBS.
Not very many, but all good ones.
BASIC PRICE - £13. 13. 0.
with seat pin, head and bracket fittings complete.
NO EXTRA FOR SPECIAL DESIGN.
More expensive filaments and elaborate finish charged extra at current prices.

OUR WHEEL BUILDING.
We have made a study of wheel building and profess to build the finest wheels ever. OUR STOCKS include all touring and racing requirements, sprints, tubulars, C/W sets, gears, handlebars, panniers, etc.
Come to the people who are qualified to deal with your wants.

WE HAVE OVER 30 YEARS' EXPERIENCE IN BICYCLE MANUFACTURE.

— **FRED PRATTS, OF, SALFORDS** —

Figure 28 Taken from the Crawley Wheelers' News mid 1950's.

Figure 29 The original head transfer

---

ber of what he felt were somewhat amateurish transfers he reluctantly accepted them. They have stood the test of time however, and are still available from John Wolfson.[11]

The second head transfer design was based upon a horse shoe, though whether this held a particular place in Fred's or perhaps Joan's hope for their new enterprise is not known. It is shown in Figure 31, whilst the full colour view can be seen as the background for the front cover.

In the mid '50's the aluminium head badge, which has been shown on the rear cover of this account, was introduced. The exact date of the introduction of this badge was not recorded, but at about this time a more angular design of downtube transfer shown in Figure 32 was finally produced — Fred having forgotten the earlier fiasco perhaps.

Some bikes were specified with fancier lug work and one or two lugless frames were commissioned. After 1952 Fred largely retired from frame building, and Pete Tester took over this function. Pete has said that he was never asked to build a Jack Knife, though he did rebuild a number to a more orthodox style. Before leaving this section do enjoy another of Fred's poems, this one penned for the fifth year Members Handbook of the RCC as can be seen in the 1950 Handbook advertisement shown in Figure 26. It is repeated here as

If the bulge in your Maes bends Or your Mafac Racer Brakes Bring them in, we weld things up And put bent things back straight.

If your head feels tight or loose Or if you've a ball or two worn out We can always put you right Just you give us a shout!

Figure 30 The earliest downtube transfers.

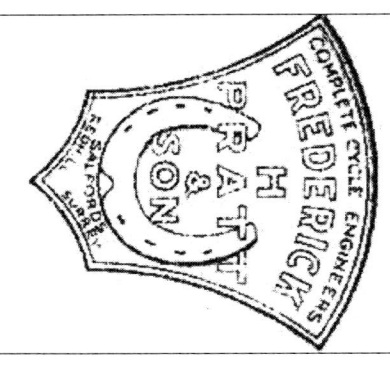

Figure 31 Shows the transfer cover for the second design of head badge.

Figure 32 The later style of downtube transfers

Working in the shop

The story of the shop's development has to be seen of course against the prevailing social and market conditions in the United Kingdom during the early post war years. The firm was slightly late, but not too late, to catch the immediate post war resumption of the cycling and outdoors pastimes boom that first started in the mid 1930's. The economic upturn was fairly slow to come but it gradually unfolded and people's expectations with it. As the shop opened, earning power was rising and interests in international sport had been resumed. As the UK market recovery was earlier than that in the devastated European countries, so keen cyclists in UK were better supplied by the plethora of small and medium sized cycle industry companies than they had been before the war. Many of these companies had learnt new techniques in light alloy manipulation and the choice of the rider for components was wide. Frederick H Pratt & Son were well placed in prosperous, or comparatively prosperous Surrey, to attract an eager market.

How the shop was run

The firm depended quite a good deal on the repair and maintenance of everyday roadster bikes, with building lightweight frames being the icing on the cake. The line up in 1949 became Fred, the proprietor, in the shop, with Joan coming in on her wheels to greet the visitors whenever she could, then Pete Tester as frame builder (and gradually becoming the doyenne of the workshop), with Noel backing on general repairs and learning his trade both from Fred and from Pete. Later, after Fred's death in 1967, Noel and Joan ran the shop first jointly, then after Joan's death in 1993, Noel became sole proprietor.

Asked about why the shop never sold their own fully built bikes, Noel explained it was due to Purchase Tax, which would have added 25% to the cost, whilst spares and secondhand machines did not attract this tax. This was one reason that the firm had a useful regular stock of re-built bikes for sale. These frames carried a Frederick Pratt Reformare transfer, as shown below in Figure 33, some being simply rebadged, others a complete respray.

Apart from bikes taken in part exchange, bicycles that were of a suitable quality were sometimes bought by the shop, usually from Police lost property auctions. These would be renovated and sold on as Frederick Pratt Reformare machines. Such bikes never had a FHP & Sons number. A similar practice has been reported in a great many smaller cycle businesses at this time.

Noel recalls how in this period, it was particularly hard for keen cyclists, and many of the customers were both young and keen, to make ends meet. This is borne out by Clive Oxx's account of how he scrimped and saved for his Jack Knife frame, bought from Fred in 1952. Clive can be seen, in a splendid evocation of a fast lad out on his iron, in Figure 34. Clive still remembers Fred talking him into buying his frame.

Figure 34 Clive Oxx on his Frederick Jack Knife Applied model in 1952

Figure 33 FHP transfer used on renovated cycles of other makes.

Working in the shop

How tight the finances of the shop were can also be judged by the fact that the Army had allowed a six months delay in Noel's National Service, which ran from 1950 to 1952, in order that he could help get the shop running properly. Even then, after a few months basic training in Yorkshire, he was twice allowed home for several weeks. This was virtually compassionate leave to help out in the shop, because his role in the shop for cycle frame preparation had been acknowledged by the authorities to be important to his father's business. Noel went on thereafter to have exciting wartime experiences on the Imjin River in Korea. He wistfully recalls it was "a bit like a holiday away from the hours in the shop and work room".

It is probable that in these early days, Fred found that running the shop, training staff, and getting the shop known, was a hard enough job without making special frames for people. It was only later on that the firm's ability to build frames to customers' wishes was able to flourish – it probably did not become easy until Noel was back and another pair of hands was available sometime in late 1952. In December 1951 the shop's advertisement in Cycling[4] only referred to repairs – no house machines were offered.

The staff

The shop's first fulltime employee was Derek Pullen. Derek had grown up in River View Road, Ruxley Lane, Tolworth and came down to Salfords with the Pratt family. Derek had worked in cycle shops before, though he was younger than Fred. He did not stay with Fred for very long though, perhaps due to the low turnover and probably low pay packet at the beginning of the shop's life.

The first of the new firm's trainees, and a man who was to be truly important in the firm, was Peter Tester. Pete in time became the frame builder of the firm, taking over this role from Fred, perhaps as early as 1950 onwards. Pete was borne in 1922 in Hove, Sussex, where his father worked as a gardener, but the family moved to the Holmwood area near Dorking in the early 1930's. Pete's first job in 1937 was making aeroplane fuselage sections in a small factory at Gatwick close to the historic Gatwick 'Beehive' aerodrome building. Cycling the Surrey lanes from Dorking to Gatwick, about 12 miles each way every day, must have been very enjoyable – and would have helped build up the muscles!

Pete recalls his first real bike was a James Grose, which was reasonably light – certainly not a gas-pipe frame, though he remembers most of the components seemed to be seconds with things like non matching clips on the levers for the Monitor Climax brakes. Catastrophe struck when the frame broke under him on a ride to the South Coast. A local bike shop had a second-hand Merlin frame and Pete swapped all his components and was soon on his way again, now mounted on a hand made frame.

In these days Pete was in the Dorking Old Paulownians. He remembers his first race in 1938, a Kentish Wheelers Novice 25, on the 'Pan' course. He was pleased that he managed a 1.11, with the event won by Charlie Council in 1.7. It was through such events he met riders from the Tooting Bicycling Club which he joined after the Dorking OP's closed.

Asked about bike choices at this time he recalls a high degree of pressure on young riders to ride machines fitting in with the current fads and noted that the average keen competition rider was unlikely to ride a street machine such as a Raleigh, Hercules or Philips. Indeed he recounted the tale of a mysterious unknown rider on an Addiscombe event. This tall thin six-foot lad appeared for a 30 mile time trial with a 21 inch Raleigh "fitted with half a yard of seat pin" the bike also being fitted with road tyres. The stranger caused some amusement, and had to be talked into borrowing some 26inch high-pressure tyre wheels for the event by a friendly marshal. The tale ends, of course, with the tall stranger setting a new club record that day. The rider was Eddy Mundy, who went on to other and greater exploits. But the message of this tale is that you had to be good, really good, to get away with mundane gear and still be one of the lads.

Pete never met Fred Pratt at this time, as Fred rode for the Tooting Bec Club, which was essentially a CTC section club. Pete's racing was all done on fixed wheel bikes, working between 78 and 84 depending on the event. He remembers his Club's main racing area was the Portsmouth Road. Asked about gears Pete recalls Cyclo gears with no enthusiasm at all, regarding them as for touring and never to be used for racing. Then again, and doubtless with his later shop experience in mind, he recalls the problems of the clip-on Cyclo gears slipping round the chain-stay. Other problems with this system arose because even if slipping had been avoided by the use of Cyclo mounts being brazed onto the frame, if the owner later wanted to alter the size of the sprocket cluster, the mounts might have to re brazed.

But to return to Pete's career, after a year or so at Gatwick, he spent sometime in 1938 in the machine shop at Baker's in Dorking (now a Vauxhall garage). Then briefly joined an armaments contractor before moving to the Dorking Foundry, which made most of the manhole covers used in the town at that time. The foundry work varied, with one week the castings being made in iron and the next, in aluminium. Then the war descended.

After four years in the Army, over which Pete is strangely quiet, except that he made a number of cycling friends, including Jim Wilson of Sheffield, Pete returned home. He found himself in a number of light engineering jobs around Redhill, including, for instance, making the Schumuly Pistol rockets for signal guns and fire extinguishers in Newdigate.

32

Working in the shop

Cycling again, after the war, Pete joined the newly formed Redhill Cycle Club (RCC). In 1948/9 Pete felt in need of a new bike. A club friend, Alan Large, suggested he tried the new shop in Salfords, FHP & Son. Doubtless there were many RCC members who were introduced to the shop in this way, as the club was keen to foster Fred's shop. Fred had the same sort of background as many riders, because the RCC, though formed largely for racing, developed plenty in common with Fred's personal love of the touring bike. Fred and Joan did indeed become committee members of RCC in the early 1950's, whilst Pete himself was an active member as Secretary and Track/Team Manager in the same period.

Pete remembers his first impressions were that Fred had some interesting bronze welded frames in the shop, and there were long discussions with Fred on building techniques. These soon progressed to gentle wrangles over the specification for a frame for Pete. Fred explained the Jack Knife principles, but Pete was a young racing man with his own ideas, and did not altogether believe the elder's conjectures. Still there were compromises that could be made, and Pete remembers his new frame was 72/72 angles with 18 inch chainstays, Chater Lea bottom bracket, and Claud Butler dropouts. Figure 35 shows Noel, top, and Pete, below, in an RCC event in 1949 on his Frederick.

Either during the building of this bike, or perhaps slightly later, Pete and Noel both remember a type of subtle tea mug ceremony developing with Joan Pratt's ever ready teapot whenever Pete called in to chat on his way home in the evenings. The discussions on frame design were often animated. Somehow the question was asked, perhaps when Fred's first frame builder Derek Pullen was moving on, and then later in 1949 Pete found himself agreeing to work with the firm. Fred took Pete through a course in frame construction process and also into wheel building and so Pete became a member of the team. So much so that later that same year when his parents moved away from Dorking, Pete moved into a room in the Pratt's home above the shop. Les Surman then joined the firm, primarily to work with Fred and then with Pete as the filing assistant for the cleaning up and finishing of the frames prior to dispatch for painting.

Noel also remembers Gordon Ball who, although never employed by the firm, was a regular in the shop, and quickly impressed with his cycling prowess. Gordon was the first RCC Champion and Best All Rounder and remained so for a number of years. He and Pete Tester were very closely matched and Noel recalls how they regularly alternated as first or second in SCCU events. Gordon is still an active, though recreational only, cyclist and has only recently retired from the local cycle company CN, in Crawley.

The last of the apprentices or staff of the firm was Richard Woods. Richard joined in 1958/9 and like others, Richard was a keen cyclist and put up some good 25 mile times. He lived south of East Grinstead and Noel remembers that they were both racing at the same time. Despite the difference in ages they were well matched with Richard's time for a 25 on the home G9, the Cherry Tree, course being 23 seconds faster than Noel. Noel still gets lit up, even 'aeriated' to use his own expression, when recalling an event on the G9 route that passed the shop. Noel was off an hour before Richard and returned a time nearly 2 minutes up on his own best time. Richard went scatty (to use Noel's own phrase!) when he saw Noel's time. Richard responded however and came up with a faster time – one which left him exactly 23 seconds up on Noel!! The sheer disbelief on Noel's face must have been something to see – because you can still see it and hear it in his voice when he retells the tale some forty years later.

Figure 35 Noel, above, and Pete Tester below in their competition days

Noel remembers most of this life as if it were yesterday, and his words would carry a graphic description of the realities of life in the cycle trade in the fifties and then later in the sixties after the motor car had become established and cycling entered one of its doldrums.

Noel recalls how Fred, out in the front of the shop, would encourage customers to buy one of his stock frames or to have a frame built especially for them. Once he had made a sale, he would then ask the customer to speak direct to Pete who would be called into the shop so that he could discuss the order and settle the details. Many a time it would be Noel who recorded the choices, often on the back of a suppliers receipt or whatever was available to be written on. (Some of these accidentally survived Joan's clear-out and were found in the back of a draw in the late 1990's.)

Working in the shop

It was clear even as early as 1950, that the buying customers were not too keen on the Jack Knife principles, and sadly this 'different' frame design appears not to have progressed much beyond a handful of frames Fred built up before 1949 when he was still the firm's only frame builder. (Although as there are no records it could be that Fred and Derek Pullen did produce some frames before Pete Tester was taken on in late 1949).

It is reasonably certain that numbers of Jack Knife frames were small because Pete Tester never built a Jack Knife frame himself. "I never believed in them," he says, and there was a twinkle in his eye when he said this and looked at Noel. But he did have one at one time, just shortly after starting in the shop. He was not impressed with Fred's polemics, and furthermore did not like the frame, but did note that at that time he was racing every week with a "fairly short" machine using an orthodox 72/72 frame. One suspects he was not particularly objective and fashion played its inevitable part in his choice.

Returning to everyday life at the counter, it was not, to use a quote from Noel "all Campag and Scherens rims". "Money was very, very tight, from the moment we opened" recalls Noel. "We could only just pay off the interest on our mortgage at the start. There were a number of times over the years when we could not pay our staff and Pete had to find work in a local factory at one time in the mid 1950's when things were quiet". "We had to lay off our frame builders finally after Fred died on 15 November 1967", he says and there is still a catch in his throat when he remembers the despair at that time. "My mother and I rented out the firm's workshop to them - Pete and his assistant - and they made a new career with engineering subcontracts for a further three years". "I had to move our (the shop's) repair work into the garage at the bottom of the garden and had to use that as the workshop and storeroom for many years". "Through very hard graft and 13 hour working days for a good number of years we just survived. The rent from the workshop allowed us to pay off our mortgage and for the first time in the firm's history we were not running on a credit platform."

Later on, as Joan Pratt's infirmities became greater, it took all of Noel's skills as negotiator to keep her from worrying over the business – and trying to put her own oar in. At one point Noel comments "A family business is not the cakewalk many presume it must be" and about his mother and shop affairs (after she had recovered) he said "Ignorance was bliss as far as she was concerned". This comment is made because he now knows she had for years kept the financial details from Noel in case he worried. He thinks that she was worried that if he had known more about the true financial state of the firm, after his father's death he might perhaps have tried to sell the shop over her head. Poor Joan must have been worried about what would become of her in that instance. There must have been tussles going on that the visitor to the shop

could never have been aware. There was always an air of bon hommie in the shop – or at least a good front put on by the pair – as shown in the typical shot in Figure 36 which was taken sometime in the 1970's.

Noel ends his comments on this period with – "To sum up, though, we were always a smooth, and very satisfying environment" Perhaps that was said with the benefit of distance. It was Joan, after all, who one day after Fred's death, had burnt all the firm's early accounts and shop records, presumably so that Noel would not know enough about the firm's finances. Nevertheless despite these under currents, (and of course the all pervading smell of fish being boiled for the cats!), the shop must have been a satisfying place to work in. Indeed, Noel recalls that "one employee, (Les Surman), whom we had to lay off through a long quiet spell, begged us to allow him to carry on working for us unpaid until things picked up."

Figure 36 Noel and Joan ready to serve or chat to customers in the shop in the 1970's

Working in the shop

Despite all the hardships and ups and downs in their careers, Pete Tester and Noel are still in regular contact and they and their wives provided the writer with a fascinating account of their early years together when we met to talk over this account of the firm in 2003. Figure 37 shows Pete and Noel in retirement outside Noel's home.

Figure 37 Noel Pratt and his frame builder Pete Tester in retirement in 2003.

The bikes and their riders, stories from owners' anecdotes

The trailer bike, which was the name given to Fred's experimental bicycle that would become the Jack Knife design, had extreme values of the frame design features so as to test the principle of 'Riding the front wheel.' Fred realized that this design was of course the archetypical unusual frame, and never intended it as a commercial proposition. Rather he hoped that the less extreme Jack Knife Applied would become popular. It would seem that Fred was disappointed. The non-acceptance of the Jack Knife idea seems to have been resounding and thus this experiment lasted only a short time at the beginning of his enterprise. Later commercial realities loomed large and he was content to produce high quality standard frames.

Fred had wanted a good stiff rear end and also the stiffest possible main triangle for which he used the shortest down tube and top-tube. This led to his use in the Jack Knife design, of the 1 1/8 inch tubing (more normally restricted to tandems for the tandem's 'drainpipe') for the main triangle tubes. Noel noted that at the time this choice of relatively exotic tubes was easy as they obtained their supplies of tubing from CB's, at this period, the national trade distributor for Reynolds and the vital 531 tubing; but later when Holdsworth took over that role, 531 became scarcer and a certain tightness and suspicion of trade competition made life much more difficult.

When asked about unusual requests, Pete does not recall any particularly unusual frames, apart that is from the Jack Knife frame, which was in any event before his time. He recalled building a number of frames with 12 inch top tubes for stronger riders. One particularly problematic frame was one he built for Phil Hitchcock (6113) that had a rare Stronglight taper-bearing bottom bracket. Another early 'scandal' within the shop was in the early 1950's with an American order, which had come in as a result of an advertisement by Fred in either the CTC magazine or in Cycling, or from a recommendation by the Butler family who were then living in the US. This order was for a fully chromed, filed lugged frame. The firm lost a huge amount of money, due to the high cost of construction, then the packing and transport, as Fred insisted on not passing on the true costs to the purchaser.

Both Pete and Noel remembered what became known to them as the Christmas Tree bike - obviously a bike which came up for a great deal of banter in the shop - though at this distance its owner and frame number cannot be recalled. This rider wanted every accessory going, and, in the days when adding braze-on's was thought to weaken frame strength, his touring frame had the lot, bottle cages, front and rear racks, double lamp brackets, mirrors, dynamo, gear and brake cable end stops. In-

deed it was only surpassed in its idiosyncrasy by the bike accessory for George Tickner that Noel had to construct on George's special lightweight bike - a pipe rack on the handlebars. It seems he favoured straight stem pipes - this was lucky, as a rack for a curly Petersen pipe could have been a real problem!

Although it appears that the Jack Knife model of Frederick did not survive the rigours of the market place in the early 1950's, the idea did however come round again, in that bewildering fashion so often remarked upon in the cycling world. In the early 1990's Steve Bauer, Canadian contender for Tour de France honours, was attempting to get back into a team eligible for Tour de France entry after he had had a disastrous 1992. He badly needed some extra 'Oomph' to assist his competitive comeback. So there he was early in 1993, found out by the media with his new secret weapon, a relaxed angles long wheelbase machine[12]. It had been built up for him by Eddy Merckx no less, to a design of his own assisted by a friend M Bedmenieux, and was given the title The Stealth. It was, as can be seen in Figure 38, looking uncannily like the Jack Knife. Like others before, it raised a storm of guffaws and some unkind comments, but Steve did win some early classics that year, and swore that the bike did improve his performance.

Some months later it became obvious he had not recovered his old form and indeed he faded from the scene. But was it the design that could not help him? Was it him? Was the design shown yet again to be a lemon? Or, perish the thought, had Steve, like Fred before him, seen a need for instant publicity to raise his stature in the market place and used a 'funny bike' to get it?

The beautifully built Reynolds 531 tubed rear carrier rack built by Fred and seen in Figure 18 was used as a pattern for rear racks to order on other bikes. Fred had developed the model whilst at CB's and incidentally made good use of

Figure 38 Steve Bauer and The Stealth

The bikes and their riders, stories from owners' anecdotes

his own rack when taking unwanted food from the CB canteen home to his chickens most days during the war. A similar matching saddlebag support was also made for Harry Knowles, and Harry remembers it well. He has somehow lost his Frederick 58710, but has managed to keep its special saddle bag support and proudly uses it on his current bike.

Talking of Frederick riders, both Noel and Pete recall Fred Marshall, a real hard rider who only took up cycling after the war at age 35, but who became a successful part of the RCC's team with Pete and Gordon Ball.

Bernard Pusey, who became a professional with Hercules, but who had started with RCC when he lived on Reigate Hill was a good friend and remained in touch long after he ceased to be a RCC team-mate. Pete remembers that at a race in Lee on Solent, Bernard, who was guesting as an invited rider, was baulked by a major crash at about halfway, and was picking himself up when Pete arrived. With a shout, "Jump on, Pete," Bernard helped Pete get further up the field than he would otherwise have been able to manage himself. Pete was later able to help Bernard, by building him a fast lightweight, which whisper it quietly, was then badged as a Hercules.

Then there was Arthur Wilcockson, a solicitor who lived in Dorking and who died whilst out cycling with the club. His son John Wilcockson was also a keen cyclist and became the well known cycling journalist with Sporting Cyclist as well as owning two Fredericks. John Tole now owns one of these bicycles, frame number 6512. John bought the machine second hand from Condor's in 1977. It was rebuilt but was used for many years without its head badge, which had been stolen from it whilst John was shopping one day. The badge was eventually re-badged courtesy of Noel, and is still regularly campaigned by John who is a V-CC member. A photograph of was the machine ridden by John Wilcockson to the Italian Lakes. A photograph of the bike at Lac Lucarno was published in Sporting Cyclist in 1968.

Pete recalled that Arthur Wilcockson regularly organised a Christmas Carol ride to Newbury where he knew the incumbent. A mild scam developed; with a small ancient pub acting as the base for the carolers. From this centre the cyclists made forays to the local large houses, bringing some discordant noise and much Christmas cheer, before retiring to the said pub to spend some of the wassailing takings in the bar.

Clive Oxx has kindly recorded his recollections of his "Frederick" experiences. "My first bicycle was created from a pre-war AW Cycles bicycle purchased second hand and painted by hand with Robialac enamel in a creative scheme of maroon with silver lugs. I was fourteen years of age when I turned up in 1948 at the start of a ride with the new Section of the CTC – the North Cheam Section. I did not feel welcomed as I was lectured on the unacceptability of my 'sports' bicycle of which I was so proud. It did not have mudguards and they did not approve of the colour scheme.

In 1952 I had earned sufficient to consider the purchase of a new bike. I do not know the date when I saw a fine new frame in the windows of F.H. Pratt's shop in Salfords. It had a label explaining that it was built to a special design of the owner of the business. I talked with the owner in the shop and heard about the benefits of this special design. Mr Pratt gave me a single page leaflet and I read this with interest at my home in Worcester Park. I was persuaded to buy this beautiful blue Frederick Pratt frame that would be the basis for my new bike. I kept that leaflet for a number of years but do not have it now. It's great benefit was a comfortable safe ride with none of the alarming twitching at the rear end that new steep angled bikes could produce. Sunday Club runs in those days were often 100 miles or more so comfort could be important.

It did appear to absorb road bumps and vibration very effectively. I always felt that the disadvantage was loss of forward momentum as you started up a slope and it did not feel so directly responsive on hills. There were times when you sensed that you were dragging a light trailer. This may have been my imagination however as I was not a particularly strong hill climber. I regretted that my new machine did not always provoke admiration from fellow clubmen. It's design was always unorthodox when, in a period of frame design to angles of 73/71 or 72 degrees parallel, bikes with steeper angles were increasingly favoured by faster racing men. "Why did you buy that", I was often asked. I was a member of the Kingston Phoenix Road Club when I used the Frederick Pratt for my first time trial in the Kentish Wheelers Novices 25 mile Time Trial on March 22nd in that Golden Jubilee year of 1953. I ended middle of the field of 120 riders with 1hr 11.45mins. The fastest time was 1hr 05.17mins by my great cycling companion Chris Zavos who was sadly disqualified and could not claim as winner of the event. (Figure 34 has shown Clive riding in this event.) "The bike, which I always referred to as a Frederick Pratt, did some good annual mileages. (Doubtless it had the early Frederick Pratt transfers, not the later Frederick version AJES) In my first year of a three year engagement for the RAF I rode over 12,000 miles. This included commuting on leaves from my base on Portland Bill, Dorset to home. As these were rides of 130 miles the comfort of the F.H. Pratt was helpful! When I was posted to the new NATO base in West Germany for my second year of service I applied for permission to bring my bicycle out to the base and to start, with two other airmen, a cycling club. (Note, I had a description published in F.C.O.T NEWS of the drama experienced in getting delivery to the airbase.) We were very pleased to be able to cycle out into the countryside around the base at Bruggen on the Holland/ Germany borders. I was very proud of the quality of the Frederick Pratt frame. The welded joints were perfectly finished. It was well enamelled in a mid-blue and I remember keeping this finish in gleaming state with a special Three in One pol-

37

The bikes and their riders, stories from owners' anecdotes

I purchased a Gillott with my demobilisation payment. It was a beautiful frame which I equipped with some of the top accessories of that period. I regret that I was not using it with the Pratt design when I suffered a very serious 'shimmy' accident in 2002a in which I was nearly killed. I am sure that the long wheelbase of my Frederick Pratt machine would have prevented the extreme flexing of the bottom bracket that developed such incredible force, throwing me violently on to my face and impacting my legs on to the road surface."

Clive ends his tale with "I do not recall ever previously hearing of the 'Jack Knife', even from Mr Pratt himself. My frame was to all intents and purposes a standard club frame of the day but with an extended wheelbase length to the rear triangle. However, when I spoke to Noel about it in 2002 it appears it may have been a pre-production Jack-Knife as it came without any distinguishing transfers or decorations". Clive would dearly love to recover that bike or see it again.

Tony Killick was one of Fred's young enthusiasts in the early 1950's, cycling at that time with the Crawley Wheelers Club. Figure 39 shows two action shots of the young Tony. In the upper photograph we see Tony on his Frederick, frame number 52108, in a 25mile time trial on G9 in 1952, sporting a 'Van Melson'. This was the name given by the Southern Wheelers to the hairnet, which was first copied from Vic Gibbon of Brentwood Road Club. Its name in the club came from the local ladies' hairdressers who presented the Southern Wheelers with a box of the nets; they were a-hoped-for speed aid. The club still lightheartedly awards each year the "Van Melson Trophy" for the most meritorious service to the club.

The lower picture in Figure 39 shows Tony, again in 1952, riding 79 fixed with Harden hubs, Major Taylor stem and alloy bottles at Cowfold 24 hour This machine has now been re-built by its current owner Pat Curtis and can be seen in Figure 40.

Some quotes from Noel

In finishing this story, I can't resist the temptation to recall some of the unforgettable phrases that have tripped from Noel's lips, many of which have been treasured down the years by his customers. Noel never stops talking, you have to realise, but he could be brought to a close at times. Perhaps you could suddenly hide behind a new customer, or, in the absence of one, open the shop door with signs of real conviction. Then he would relent and draw to a close, particularly as the shop door alarm would continue to ring whilst the door was kept open; he would then give you that quintessential Noel grin, and a "Cheerio" that helped to bring you back next time.

A couple of 'Noelisms' follow:-

A "All you (V-CC) chaps want is black covered Sturmey-Archer control cables, handle bar stopwatch carriers, GB brakes spares, or Chossy round saddlebags. I do try to sort you out but I can't always find them, I'm not running a ruddy museum here you know!" (More or less verbatim to Alvin Smith) But he often did find them, when not looking! Sneakingly, many of his friends and loyal customers did latterly visit Noel's museum piece shop for the very joy of what it was!

B "Well, you brought it in with a loose cotter pin and when I looked it over, as you said I should, I wished I hadn't. The one pedal was useless so I found another of the same type (you don't know how lucky you are!) in my spares box, the bottom bracket was out of kilter so I fixed that and the brake blocks were plum worn out and anyway back to front only rust holding the blocks in. I can't help it but I am afraid the bill is rather spiteful, I am so sorry." (Not verbatim, but in the spirit of Noel's explanation to Stuart Hoare).

Figure 39 Tony Killick in 1952 on Frederick 52108 now owned by Pat Curtis.

Figure 40 Frederick 58108 now restored and treasured.

Concluding remarks

I have posed a number of questions and done my best to answer some of them for this story and have pestered Noel, Pete and a number of old and new friends along the way, and it has been very enjoyable. So far Noel and Pete have agreed with my reconstructions and I am grateful to them and to the other contributors to the tale for their forbearance if I have not got it quite right. Have I got near to the truth? I hope so, but even if not I hope it has been enjoyable to read. I would like to finish with words from Graham Haysom, keen cyclist and long term RCC member.

"We will never know all the answers but I suppose the firm's legacy is the frames that still survive and the memories of those who rode them."

On that score I believe the efforts of all those involved in recording this story of the firm have been worthwhile, and I hope that together we have saved a number of old bikes from oblivion and at least started some hares running in terms of further recollections.

If any reader wishes to write to me about their own experiences with Frederick bicycles, or with other information about the firm, I shall be happy to add to the text.

References

These are reproduced in Appendix D, courtesy of Mr P N (Noel) Pratt

[1] *TS Wallace* — *Cycling and Sporting Cyclist* 7 June 1969
[2] *CB* — *The CB catalogue* 1939
[3] *T. Lane* — Conversation with Tom Lane 15 November 2002. I have not seen these.
[4] *cycling* — Advertisement in classified ads in edition for 13 December 1951
[5] *FHP&S* — The four brochures are :
  1. *The Jack Knife position* - 2 pages for 4d
  2. *Pedalling a bicycle efficiently* – 5 pages for 4d
  3. *Progress of Design* – 10 pages for 4d
  4. *Positioning with a purpose* – 22 pages for 6d
[6] *Fearnley C* — *Your Build and your bicycle Cycling* November 19 1947
[7] *Cohen I* — *Fashions in Frame Angles: Are steep angles necessary? Cycling* January 31 1952 page 119.
[8] *CB adverts* — *Cycling* most years there were annual events such as Claud's Do
[9] *Burrows* — *Bicycle Design*, Company of Cyclists Publications 2001. Pages 34/35
[10] *Redhill CC* — *Members's Handbooks for the years 1949 to 1957*
[11] *J Wolfson* — J.Wolfson Esq, 15 Willow Ridge, Turners Hill, Crawley, West Sussex, RH10 4PN.
[12] *Cycling* — 13 December 1951 page 14
[13] *R Guinness* — *No laughing matter- Steve Bauer and the Stealth bike. Cycling Weekly* April 24 1993

APPENDIX A

The list of frames shown in Table A1 has been taken from the informal shops list of custom frames maintained by Noel Pratt once he had returned form National service in 1952 using his then already out of date 1949 Electrical Engineers diary. Figure B1 below shows the first entry page of the list, which was at the back of the diary (starting with G. Elder 5121), whilst on the left page and now upside down his notes of his first cycle races can be seen.

Not all the frames were recorded by Noel. Thus Pat Illing had bought his first frame 4911, well before Noel's records begin apparently in February 1951. Frame 4971 was taken in part exchange by Geoff Littler in his shop in Penzance and recently purchased by Alvin Smith. Pat Illing also bought from the Salfords shop in the 1990's, an un-restored second-hand bike. This bike, number 5959, was also a non-recorded frame number. Malcolm Bainbridge bought his frame 593064 in 1959 or 1960 from the shop for around £17 guineas, this was a shop stock frame chosen from a number hanging in the shop. All four of these numbers have been added to the list in Table B1 to make it also a full register of known frames but these four have been shown in italics to separate them for noels original data.

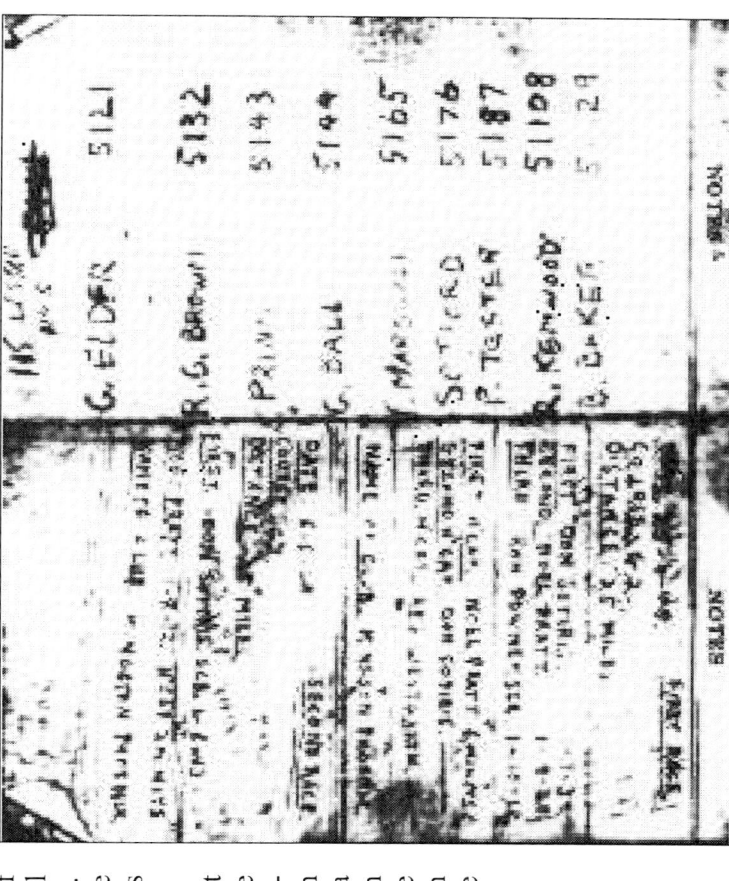

Figure A1 shows the Old diary "Notes" page entry where Noel recorded the FHP frames, now the only record remaining.

APPENDIX A

Table A.1 List of Frederick frames taken from listing kept by Noel Pratt

Frame	First owner	Current owner	Details, history where known	Form
4911	Pat Illing			
4971	-	Sold in France	JK lugless T/T 1¼WB 44½, 1952 converted to Φh	No
5121	G. Elder	AJE Smith	Taken in p/e by Geoff Littler Penzance	
5132	R.G. Brown			No
5143	Prince			
5144	Gordon Ball			
5165	Fred Marshall	PC crashed	Sold to P Crowsley 1962, remains with Tony Killick	
5176	Setford			
5187	P. Tester		RCC member, main frame builder in FHPS	
51108	R. Kenwood			
51129	B. Baker		Noel's future wife	
5211	L. Surman		RCC member, also in the firm	
5222	R. Westgarth		Joan's brother and RCC member	
5223	Fred Marshall		RCC member	
5244	Pat Illing		22½, Lugless T/T=1¼, Angles 67/68, 2¼ rake	No
5265	T. Woods			
5266	Shop stock		Tandem	
5297	D. Rowe			
52108	Tony Killick	Pat Curtiss	Racing history, rebuilt by PC given by TK	
52109	Fred Marshall		May be bike owned by P Crowsley, written off	
521110	Pete Tester			
521211	Gordon Ball			
5311	O. Wyles		Olive was RCC Ladies Champion	
5312	C. George			
5323	Noel. Pratt		May have been track ends later sold to …….	
5334	G. Hoare			
5335	H. Pratt		Not known as family, but may Fred's brother	
5346	Perryman			
5347	Johnson			
5348	Ken Bean			
5349	Pete Tester			
53510	Rossier			
53611	J. Taylor		Tandem, still around in Copthorne?	
53612	Reynolds			
5411	Shop stock			
5412	Lightfoot			
5413	A. Hoare			
5414	Scott			
5415	Pete Tester			
5426	Shop stock			
5427	Greenwood			
5438	Willett			
5439	Gordon Ball			
54310	Batsford			
54311	Scott			

Frame	First owner	Current owner	Details, history where known	Form
54412	D. Rowe			
54413	G. Hoare			
54514	Miss Bristow			
54815	A. Large			
541016	Bryant			
541117	Pete Tester			
5511	W. King			
5532	CTC		Display model for exhibition	
5533	P. Tester			
55124	Smith			
5611	J.Theyers			
5622	G. Rooke			
5633	Barnes			
5654	Greenwood			
5656	G. Powney			
5731	P. Tester			
5752	J. Poat		Ordered by Mr Batchelor	
5763	Miss Ware			
5764	P. Tester			
5795	K. Stokes			
5796	J. Poat			
5811	P. Illing		For Mrs Illing Angles 69/69	No
5812	Rowe			
5813	Smithers			
5814	Hollands			
5815	D Dumbrill			
5816	P. Tester			
5827	Black	J Wolfson	Track frame single fixed	
5843	Tickner			
5859	Rodgers			
58710	H Knowles		Saddle support in 531 still exists	
58911	Chilicott			
581012	P. Tester	AJE Smith	Pete's bike gifted to & rebuilt by AS 2003 Ex P Crowsley, 21frame fancy lugs, race/tourer	Yes
581113	Robinson	J Wolfson		
581114	Leaney		Taken by Leaney to New Zealand	
581115	Lunn			
581216	Klepzig			
581217	Dumbrill			
5911	Fabb			
5912	Pendreith			
5913	Gilbert			
5934	Boulter			
5935	R. Wood			
5936	Wicks			
5947	Shop stock			
5948	D Dumbrill			
5949	Shop stock			
5959	Pat Illing	Pat Illing	Bought S/H from shop in 1990's	No

APPENDIX A

Frame	First owner	Current owner	Details, history where known	Form
59610	Maycock			
59611	N.P. Pratt			
59712	K. Bean			
59813	Dobson			
59914	Fabb		Noted to be Fabb's second bike	
59915	Shop stock			
59916	Burrells			
591117	Roberts			
591118	Wright			
591119	Jurville			
591220	A. White			
591221	D. Ward			
591222	Seymour			
593064	M Bainbridge	M Bainbridge	23 501 Reynolds Pratt Special, Nervex Pro	No
6011	Pete Smithers		21½ Est=£13.13.0, Actual £16.8.9	Yes
6022	Wilson			
6023	Ashdown		May have been sold to Robinson	
6024	Shop stock			
6025	Barnett			
6036	Gandee			
6037	Stokes			
6058	James			
6071	Seeley		Lugless	
60710	Phipps			
60711	Turk		Ladies frame	
60812	Standard			
60813	Standard			
60814	Sutton			
60815	Pete Tester		21	Yes
60816	Wilson			
601017	J. Corsini		Track frame	
601018	J. Corsini			
601119	Shop stock			
601120	Turner			
6111	Joel Cosham		23¾	Yes
6112	Ward			
6113	Hitchcock	P Hitchcock		
6114	Pat Curtis	Pat Curtis	Delivered March 1961 Est £14.7.0	
6115	Black			Yes
6116	Gent		23	Yes
6117	Elms		24, Ruby flam,black hd,Est £13.15.0, Fin £14.7.0	Yes
6118	Malcolm Turnbull		22¾	Yes
6119	Brian Mc Cracken		21½	
6120	Pete Smithers			Yes
6121	R Marchant			
6122	Fred Marshall		23	Yes
6123	K Till		23	Yes
6124	Pendrick		23	Yes
6125	Brenda		Pete Tester's wife	
6126	A. Nicoll		21½ Track, Front forks all chrome, frame yellow	Yes
6127	Jones		22	Yes
6128	Gould			Yes
6129	Shop stock		Sold to Golden, Hellyett green, white band on ST	Yes
6130	Noel Pratt			Yes
161	Shop stock			
261	Shop stock			
361	Shop stock		22	Yes
6131	A. Meek		22 Yellow, Lugs lined	Yes
6132	Bob Black		25 Deposit of £5 paid, Yellow+ red crown	Yes
6133	Rayland		22½ Wanted 9.2.66,	Yes
6211	Ron Ford		23 Flam red	
6212	Roy O'Donnell			Yes
6213	Shop stock			Yes
6214	Terry Grainger			
6215	Shop stock		23	
6216	Noel.Pratt	Noel Pratt	23 Mafac C/P brakes, road bike sold to Crowsley	No
6217	Colin Burrell		25 'For heavy camping	Yes
6218	K.Jackson		22	Yes
6219	Roy O'Donnell		22 Track 'For middle of September' Flam amber	Yes
6220	Mrs Gould	Colin Heath	21 Ordered by Mr H Gould 27.7.62, Plum flam	Yes
6221	C.Hopkins		24½	Yes
6311	Ian Davidson		24	Yes
6312	Pat Wilson		24 Deposit 16.1.63, Chr ends,White, blue hd,	Yes
6313	Fowler		23½ Ordered 9.2.63, Brilliant blue flam	Yes
6314	Stan Vygus		23	Yes
6315	Pat Illing	Pat Illing?	Lugless, T/T 1¼, WB=42	Yes
6316	Stephen. Smith		22 ordered 14 3.63, Brill Blue flam Fin £18.3.3	Yes
6411	Turnbull		22¾ Drawing of frame given, Silver flam,wh hd	Yes
6412	Dave Dyer		22	Yes
6413	Trussler		23¼ Old gold, lugs lined	Yes
6414	JohnWilcockson		23	Yes
6415	Peter Head		24	Yes
6416	MartinMcIllvery		23½	Yes
6417	Geoff Boxall		22¼ Ruby Lustre, note to Pete on accessories	Yes
6418	Howard Burrell		23	Yes
6419	Johnson		22 Lived in Hove	Yes
6420	John Pratt		Not family,lived inCharlwood Dawes green frame	Yes

43

APPENDIX A

Frame	First owner	Current owner	Details, history where known	Form
6511	W Tucker		23	Yes
6512	John Wilcockson	J Tole	22½ JW initials in Gold, Fin=£18.15.0	Yes
6513	Bill Heron		24½, Blue lustre, Dk blue hd, Est=£17.17.0	Yes
6514	Peter Head			Yes
6515	Brian McCracken		21½ May have been a stock frame customized	Yes
6516	David Edwards		22½ Flam green, white head, Est=£19.7.0	Yes
6517	Mrs French		20 Ladies open frame	Yes
6611	Roy Stevens		21½ Light blue, Est=£17.5.0	Yes
6612	R Taylor		24, 2.3.66 Crimson Frame £17.17.0 Bike Fin £52.17.0	Yes
6613	Charlie Burrell		23 Gold flam name on TT	Yes
6614	Peter Head		23½	Yes
6615	Hart		25 inch frame initially stock, then sold to Hart	Yes
271	Shop stock		21 inch frame 27 inch wheels	
272	Shop stock		21 inch frame 27 inch wheels	
273	Shop stock		21 inch frame 27 inch wheels	
274	Shop stock		21 inch frame 27 inch wheels	
275	Shop stock		21 inch frame 27 inch wheels	
276	Shop stock		21 inch frame 27 inch wheels	
277	Shop stock		21 inch frame 26 inch wheels	
2611	Shop stock		20 inch frame 26 inch wheels	
2612	Shop stock		20 inch frame 26 inch wheels	
2613	Shop stock		20 inch frame 26 inch wheels	
2614	Shop stock		20 inch frame 26 inch wheels	
2615	Shop stock		20 inch frame 26 inch wheels	
2616	Shop stock		20 inch frame 26 inch wheels	
6616	Hart Snr.			
6711	CF Freeman		24½TT sloping down to head tube French blue	Yes
6712	H Searl		23 inch 5.2.67	Yes
6713	Knight		24 inch	Yes
6714	J. Pratt		John not family. The last frame built.	Yes

APPENDIX B

Notes

The data in the table that follows have been extracted from three bundles of the shop's frame build notes which were found in the back of a drawer when the shop was emptied in 2002. They were given by Noel to his old friend Colin Heath. Colin has generously made them available to this study so that their historic interest can be shared with others. Although a high proportion of the build notes include pump, light and gear plus brake cable stop braze-ons, I have not included these minutae in these extracts. Please forgive this oversight.

Two representative build notes are shown in Figures C.1 and C.2, whilst Figure C.3 shows the shop's general advertising hand bill and a list of prices from 1962, more or less the period in which these particular records apply. These notes can be cross referenced with the more complete frame order records of Appendix B, which are the notes made by Noel. As a matter of convenience I have added information on paint finish and price with the Appendix B data.

Some features of the frames can be seen in the data.

1. *Nervex Pro* lugs were most commonly used with the plainer *Nervex Negere* much less popular and the even plainer *Prugnat* lugs not coming in use at least by this shop until 1964.

2. *Brampton Alatet* headsets were popular when the records start in 1958 and continue until 1963 when *TDC Continental* took over the English made sets, with small numbers of *Compagnolo* sets throughout the period.

3. The period around 1958 saw centre-pull brakes become more popular than side-pulls.

4. *Stronglight* seems the most popular bottom brackets set in the period.

5. *Campagnolo* drop-outs seemed the clear favourite either of the shop or of the customers.

6. 10 speed systems appear not to have been asked for before about 1962.

7. Looking at the build records, the only characteristic specified by all the customers was the seat tube length, otherwise sometimes the front fork rake, at other times the fork length and for others the height of the bottom bracket was included, and similarly brake sets or wheel hubs are set down. One suspects that some of this variation in the characteristics specified was that many customers would have been happy to allow the shop staff to settle these

details in their normal way. However it might also represent the fact that the shop had no formal 'tick list' to go through when a customer came in, and therefore which characteristics were ordered depended on who took the order (Fred, Noel, Pete or Joan) or how much of a hurry the customer was in at the time. Fred's and later Noel's shop was not an easy one to leave!

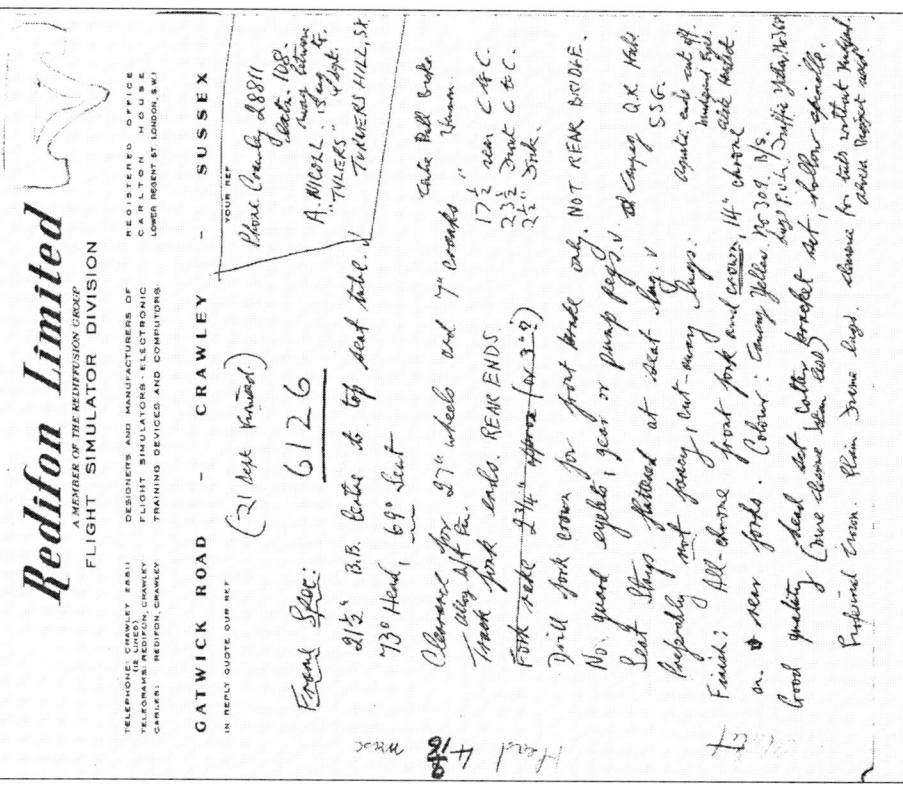

Figure C1 A build note for frame 6126 for Mr A Nicoll. This is probably made on headed paper from Mr Nicoll's employer.

APPENDIX B

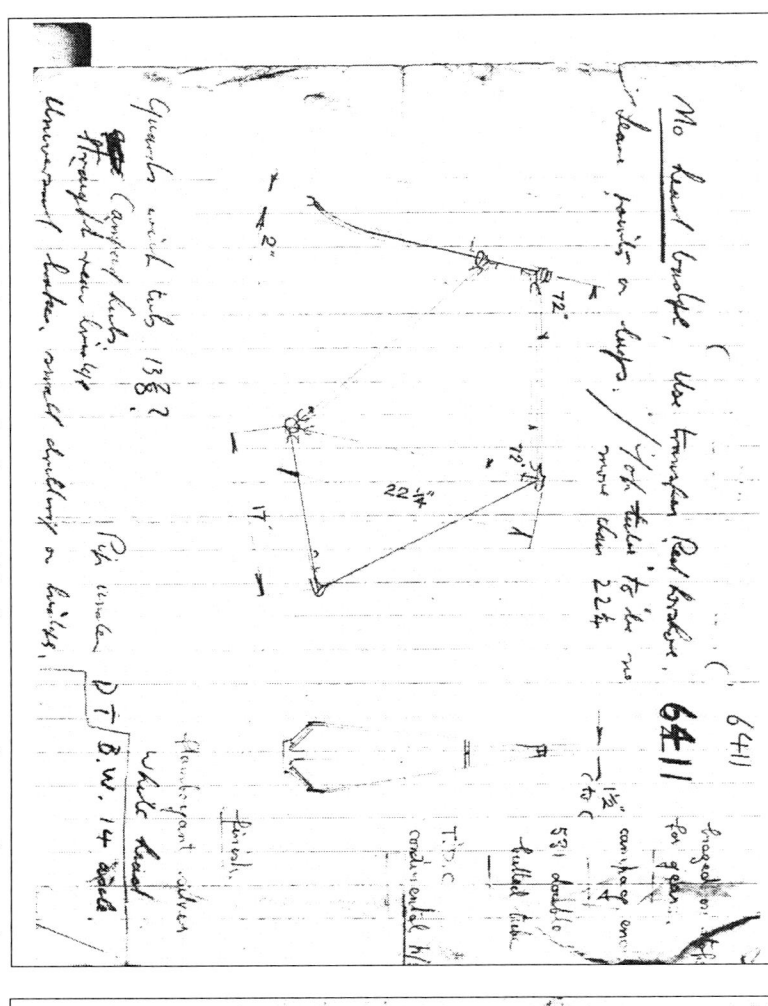

Figure C2 Another build note, this for frame 6411 where again the specification has been thought out by the customer beforehand.

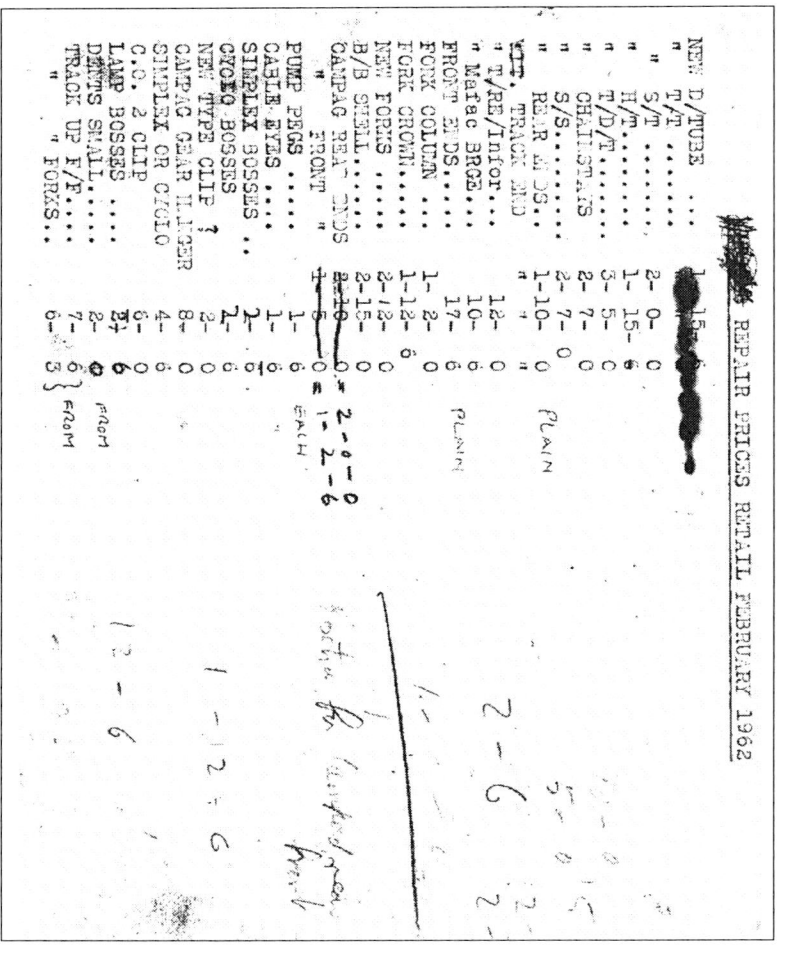

Figure C3 The firms price list for frame work in 1962 – taken from a Witcomb Cycles original

B1 Build data for Frederick frames from listing recovered from the workshop when the shop was cleared.

Frame No	Type	Seat tube	Top tube	Down tube	Fork rake	Fork length	BB ht	BB type	Head set	Head Angle	Seat angle	Chain stay	Seat stay	Brakes Type	Dropout	Hubs	Other
581113		21			2¼			BWCart	Campag	72	73			Racer	Campag	Campag	
60815		21	20¾		1¾	13⅝	10¾			72	74						Modn
6011		21½			2		10⅝		Alatet	73	73	17¼					WB40¾
6111		23¼			2	14⅛	10¾		Campag					Mafac	Campag	Campag	
6116		23			2¼	14⅛	10¾	Strong				17¼		W999	Campag		
6117		24			2¼				Alatet					W999	Campag		
6118		22¾	22⅜			13¾	10¾			72	72	17¼		Racer		Campag	
6120		21½	22⅞		2⅛	14	10¾	Strong	Alatet			17½	Wrap Ov	Campag	Simplex		
6122		23			2	14⅛ SI	10¾		Campag	72	72	17¼				Campag	WB41½
6123		23				14¼			Alatet	72	72				SA		
6124		23			2⅛				Campag	72	73			SP	Campag	CRecord	
6126		21½			2½				Alatet	72	69	17½		No rear	Agrati Tr		
6127		22					10¾		Campag	73	74	17		Uni CP	Campag	FB	WB 40½
6128		22			2	14			Alatet	73	74	17½		SP	Campag	FB	Nervex Pro
6129		23							Campag	73	73			Mafac	543	Campag	
6130		22			2		11			73	74	17½					WB40½
6131		22			2¼			Strong		72	72			Mafac		Campag	
6132		22	22		2	Round	10⅝	Strong	TDCCon	73	73	17		Mafac	Campag	Campag	
6133		25	22½		2⅜	Oval	10½	TDC	Campag	73	71	17½	Wrap Ov	Mafac		FB	
6211	Road	22½			1¼	14			Alatet	73	73					FB	N.Pro
6212	TT	23	22¼		2⅛	13⅞			Alatet	73	72½			Racer	Campag	Campag	N.Pro
6214	Road	23	22		1¾	Oval			Alatet	73	73						N.Negere
6215	Stock	22½				14⅛											
6217	Tourer	25		Hd 7⅜													
6218		22		10 sp	2⅛	13⅞			Campag	72	73½			W999			10sp on bar
6219	Track	23	22		1¾	⅝round			Alatet	72	75			Fr. SP	Simples	Airlite	N. Negere
6220		21			2⅛	14			Alatet			17¼		GB CP	Campag		N. Pro,40½
6221	Road	24½			2¼					73	71				Cyclo		N. Pro
6311		24		Hd 6⅜		14⅛			Campag	73	71				Campag		
6312	TT	24		Hd 6⅜				Strong	Alatet	73	72			W999	Campag	Airlite	Chro' ends
6313		23½						Strong						Uni CP	Campag		N Pro
6314	Road	23	22⅜					Strong	Campag	73	73	17½			Sim Cam		N Negere
6316	Road	22			2	14			Alatet					Wein		Campag	N. Pro
6411		22¼			2			BW14	TDCCon	72	72	17		Uni SP			N. Pro
6412		22			2⅛		10¾		Campag	72	72			Mafac	Campag		Prugnat
6413		23¼			2¼					72	72	17½		CP	Campag		
6414		24	22½		2		10⅞	Strong	Campag	73	72	18	Wrap Ov	CP	Campag		

APPENDIX B

Frame No	Type	Seat tube	Top tube	Down tube	Fork rake	Fork length	BB ht	BB type	Head set	Head angle	Seat angle	Chain stay	Seat stay	Brakes Type	Dropout	Hubs	Other
6416		23¼	21⅜		2⅛					73	73½			Mafac	Campag		N Pro
6417		22½	22		2	14	10¾	Strong	BW cart	72	74	17		Mafac	Simplex		
6418		23	22⅛					Strong		73	73	17¼		Uni CP	Cyclo		N. Pro
6419	Tourer	22¼			2	14	10¾		TDC Ital	72	72	17½	WB 41	Mafac	Campag		N. Pro
6420		23¼	22½		2¼			Strong	Alatet			17½	WB41¼	Driver	Campag	Haden L	
6511					2 1/16				TDC	72	72			Mafac	Campag	Campag	N. Pro
6512		23	22½		2		10¾	Strong	Campag	72	72						N. Pro
6513	Road	24½		10 sp				Strong	Campag	73	72			Mafac			N. Pro
6514																	
6515		21½	21½		2⅛	13⅞			TDC Ita	72	73			Racer	Campag	Campag	Prugnat
6516	Tour	25	22½	10 sp			10⅝	C34 cw	Campag	72½					Campag		
6517	Tour	20			2⅜	14⅜						17½	WB41½				
6611	Road	21½										17	WB 40¾		Campag		Prugnat
6612	Road	24		10 sp				Cottered	TDCCon	72	72			W999	SA	FB SF	
6613		23						Strong		73	73					Campag	
6614		23½		Hd 6⅝										Mafac	Campag		N. Pro
271	Stock	21	Wheel	27 in		BSA chr									Continent		
272	Stock	21	Wheel	27 in		BSA chr									Continent		
273	Stock	21	Wheel	27 in		BSA chr									Continent		
274	Stock	21	Wheel	27 in		BSA chr									Continent		
275	Stock	21	Wheel	27 in		BSA chr									Continent		
276	Stock	21	Wheel	27 in		BSA chr									Continent		
277	Stock	21	Wheel	27 in		BSA chr									Continent		
2611	Stock	20	Wheel	26 in		Chevron									CL rear		
2612	Stock	20	Wheel	26 in	26 in	Chevron									CL rear		
2613	Stock	20	Wheel	26 in		Chevron									CL rear		
2614	Stock	20	Wheel	26 in		Chevron									CL rear		
2615	Stock	20	Wheel	26 in		Chevron									CL rear		
2616	Stock	20	Wheel	26 in		Chevron									CL rear		
6711	10sp	24½		Rr slope	2⅛				TDCCon	73	72			W CP	Campag	Campag	N. Pro
6712	5sp	23			2	14		Strong 7		73	73			W CP	Campag	Record	N, Pro
6713		24	22⅜		2⅛			6¾	Italn	73	72			W SP	Italn	Campag	
6714	Track	22½	22¼		1¾				Italn	73	74			W SP	Italn	Record	

APPENDIX C

This appendix contains reproductions of the four Leaflets published by by FHPratt & Son sometime 1948-9. The quality of some of the originals, some of which are photocopies, is poor.

There is also a single page flyer entitled Children & Bicycles extolling the benefits of cycling for children

1	**The Jack Knife Position**	**50**
2	**Pedalling a bicycle Efficiently**	**52**
3	**Progress of Design**	**57**
4	**Positioning with a Purpose**	**63**

Children & Bicycles **74**

APPENDIX C

Leaflet No. 1   Price 4d.

We learn by Teaching

The Jack-Knife Position

A revolutionary method of cycling,

it closes the angle as closing a

"JACK-KNIFE."

by

FREDERICK H. PRATT & SON,
M.I.CYC.T.

Complete Cycle Engineers

BRIGHTON ROAD, SALFORDS,
REDHILL - - SURREY.

TELEPHONE : HORLEY 1163

———

agents for

CLAUD BUTLER, RALEIGH INDUSTRIES, Etc.

———

A Comprehensive stock of all Cyclists' needs.

THE JACK-KNIFE POSITION

THE SHAPE OF THE BICYCLE.

Seat position well behind the bottom bracket, brought close to the front wheel by short top and down tubes.

Low handlebar NOT extended forward.

Moderately well raked flexible front fork.

Long rear triangle placing rear wheel well back.

THE PART IT PLAYS.

By sloping the seat tube, the rider is seated well behind the bottom bracket and is pulling on unextended low handlebars. From this position the angle between the power push of the legs and the pull of the arms is closed. (The arms are in tension and the legs are in compression.) The weight of the body is on the legs and adds to their downward movement. This position brought forward increases the spring of the fork by the closeness of the rider's weight.

The construction of the rear triangle is rigid in all directions, and will remain so in spite of considerable lengthening, thus holding the rear wheel quite positively well back.

Sideways movement of the bottom bracket (Pendulum Action) is overcome by the presence of the short stiff down tube. The effect of such stresses being conveyed directly to the head and from there absorbed by the fork flexibility, the rear wheel being well out of harms way.

THE THEME.

When the rider's instinctive movements are allied to construction of sound design, the maximum result is obtained for the minimum physical effort expended.

Pushing with the legs and pulling with the arms is perhaps the most natural way of expending human energy. When lifting a weight, or rowing a boat as in riding a cycle, the legs are in

APPENDIX C

THE OPPOSITE TO THE JACK-KNIFE POSITION

THE SHAPE OF THE BICYCLE.

Seat position well over the bottom bracket.

Shallow fork rake.

Long top and bottom down tubes with extended handlebar.

Plenty of toe clearance.

Short rear triangle.

THE PART IT PLAYS.

By setting the seat tube upright the rider is directly over the bottom bracket. Pulling from this position, on a handlebar pushed forward by a long extension, opens the angle between the power push and pull of the legs and arms throwing the weight of the body forward onto the handlebar.

This position pushed back by the long top and down tubes removes the influence of the rider's weight from the front wheel, causing excessive sideways movement of the bottom bracket (PENDULUM ACTION) this condition being aggravated by the long whippy down tube and rigid front fork.

Every movement of the rider is directed straight to the rear wheel, by way of the very short rear triangle. The rear wheel will jump and dance from side to side resulting in considerable frictional loss between tyre and road, at the same time upsetting the balance and causing the rider to sway and wobble all over the place.

THE THEME.

Watch the rear wheel of the sprinters.

We leave the rest to your imagination.

---

compression and the arms in tension. Natural instincts can be developed to advantage forming good habits but bad habits are also formed and these can be nothing but a disadvantage. We see evidence of these habits daily among the thousands of cyclists on our roads.

The "JACK KNIFE SYSTEM" is based upon the combination of the natural instincts in harmony and practised to form good habits only. The first essential is, in effect, to ride the front wheel. Positioned forward, close up to the wheel every movement of the body plus the bumps in the road flexes the front fork causing the front wheel to bounce and work all the time. These bounces can be turned to good advantage by directing the wheel sideways before it returns to the ground, enabling the rider to manoeuvre the machine with little or no wheel turning. THIS IS THE MEANING OF RIDING THE FRONT WHEEL. It allows the toes to considerably overlap with complete safety.

Nervous riders are wise to be cautious of toe catching, but should not lose sight of the advantage gained after a little practice in riding the front wheel. The extent of the overlap should be decided by the individual, remembering that speed and efficiency is increased by drastic application of this method.

Speed increases the springing of the fork.

There is safety in speed.

APPENDIX C

Leaflet No. 2   Price 4d.
Copyright applied for.

We learn by Teaching

Pedalling a Bicycle Efficiently

Recommended in Conjunction with

THE "JACK-KNIFE" POSITION

See Leaflet No. 1

by

FREDERICK H. PRATT & SON,
F.I.CyC.T.

Complete Cycle Engineers

BRIGHTON ROAD, SALFORDS,
REDHILL - - SURREY.

TELEPHONE : HORLEY 1185

agents for

CLAUD BUTLER, RALEIGH INDUSTRIES, Etc.

———

A Comprehensive stock of all Cyclists' needs.

PEDALLING A BICYCLE EFFICIENTLY

Every cyclist is familiar with the term "ankling" in relation to turning the pedals of a cycle. This movement is undoubtedly good exercise and should be practised as such but too much indulgence in this practice may not lead to the achievement of the best results.

With mechanically propelled cranks, top and bottom dead centres are a bogey which can never be entirely eliminated but can be minimised by the use of flywheels. The dead centres occur when the crank is in a direct line with the force driving it, progress then being in the balance, a reverse or backward movement may take place. The flywheel, by means of its spinning weight, carries the crank past these vital points. Technically, this is known as "a force of zero moment." As the crank moves away from these positions the condition is then known as "the moment of force possessing magnitude," and this magnitude increases as the distance between the two points widens. This increase occurs on the downward path until it reaches the position of 3 o'clock on the face of a clock. (See diagram 1.) The force has then been multiplied on its way by 5 minutes, 10 minutes and intermediately to 15 minutes. From the 3 o'clock position to the 6 o'clock position, the magnitude decreases again and the clock must be read at 10 minutes, 5 minutes back to zero at the 6 o'clock position. On the second half of the crank rotation, from 6 o'clock to 12 o'clock, the same increase and subsequently decrease is experienced. For a simple explanation of this action see the diagram below.

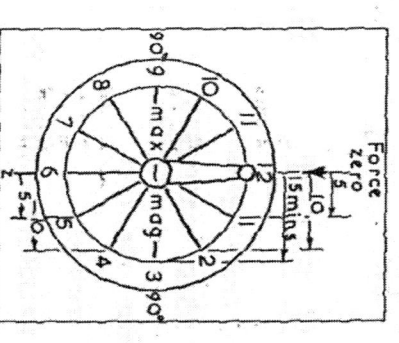

Diagram No. 1
THE MECHANICAL CRANK

APPENDIX C

A survey shows us that with the cranks at positions 3 o'clock and 9 o'clock the magnitude of the moment is at its maximum and is measured by the entire length of the crank which lies at 90 degrees to the direction of force. Positions 6 o'clock and 12 o'clock are therefore dead centres being zero moments. A person riding a bicycle can be likened to a two-piston engine but because the person has the advantage of a brain we can add an initial advantage over a mere engine and by governing the power expended by thought achieve the most efficient results possible.

Efficient results can best be defined by saying that efficiency is the act of obtaining the best result for the least possible effort and therefore in our training we must consider not only muscle strengthening but also the controlling of the mind to use natural strength economically and at the time when additional strength is most needed.

Tactical riding, whether endurance tests, sprinting or stalling, consists of developing various styles of turning the pedals, varying at will the intensity and method to achieve the best results. From a standing start or from slow to fast riding, the principle is the same. The natural method of turning the pedals is the thrusting method which can be likened to the piston rod of an engine and this can only result in one thing—a slogging match between the will of the rider and a rapid and ever mounting feeling of fatigue. To improve upon this tiring basic method of riding try the following experiment. As the left leg thrusts down pull hard on the left handlebar and at the same time exert an upward pull with the right foot holding the bar on that side tensely. Reverse the proceedure as the right foot travels down. This method you will find will give good results on the get-away but it will be found more difficult to make the change from side to side as the speed of the movement increases. To appreciate the full advantage of this method more fully, choose a steep gradient and try the experiment again.

As simple as cycle riding may seem, the style of the riding outlined in the previous paragraphs is but one of the methods of turning the pedals and for purposes of reference should be known as THE THRUSTING ACTION. Chief uses of this method being quick get-away and in hill climbing.

The next action to be studied provides the rider with sprint winning possibilities and embodies four other actions which occur as changes during the complete revolution.

The CIRCULAR or CAT'S CLAW ACTION as it should be known, can best be explained and practised by studying the first two movements of the four and then combining the remaining two movements to complete the action.

Briefly, the four movements embodied in the complete Circular Action consist of four quite separate actions which occur during the passage of the crank through a complete revolution of 360 degrees. The movements are:—

1. An upward pull at the back and at the same time with the other foot the second action—
2. A downward push at the front.
3. A forward push over the top of the circular action and at the same time with the other foot the fourth action—
4. A backward pull under the circle.

Both feet are, of course, used together and the movements changed from side to side. The object of this is to take advantage of the entire length of the crank during the complete turn or revolution. By this means, we use the maximum magnitude all the time thus removing as far as is humanly possible the "dead centre bogey."

To discover the source of power required for the second two of the four movements, another experiment is necessary. Sit in a chair with the legs extended forward to their full length and with a weight attached to one foot. It will be clearly noticed that any attempt to raise the foot which is weighted, will cause the other foot to press down against the floor in an attempt to assist the lifting of the weighted foot from the floor. No force will be operating in line with the extended legs but at right angles to them. Power should be applied to the pedals in exactly the same way, the natural lift experienced by the one leg as the lift or downward push of the other leg takes place should be accentuated to assist the complete revolution. In the correct sequence of the Circular Action, we have a push down at the front of the movement and an accentuated pull up at the back of the movement with the opposite leg. Next we have a kick forward over the top of the movement and at the same time with the other leg an accentuated kick back on the underneath section of the movement. Unlike the weight lifting movement which we found in our experiment, the movements on a cycle must be applied in a circular path and the pulls and kicks represent direction only.

Having dealt briefly with the CIRCULAR ACTION as a whole, we must now study the four separate movements and with the aid of the diagrams below learn exactly when each separate movement takes place in order that we can practice the whole action to attain riding perfection.

The four actions are named for recognition and are arranged in a clockwise direction.

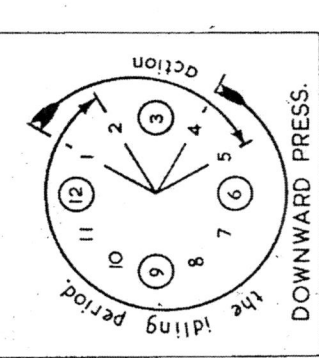

Diagram No. 2

DOWNWARD PRESS

Operating between 7½ and 22½ minutes past 12 o'clock

APPENDIX C

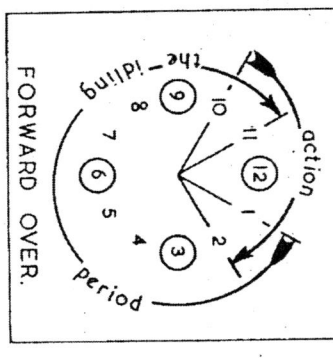

Diagram No. 3
THE BACKWARD UNDER ACTION.
Follows the Downward Press and operates between the half hour and 27½ minutes to 12 o'clock.

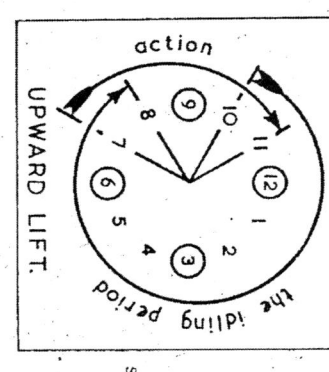

Diagram No. 4
THE UPWARD LIFT ACTION.
Operates between 27½ minutes and 7½ minutes to 12 o'clock following smoothly between the second and the fourth action.

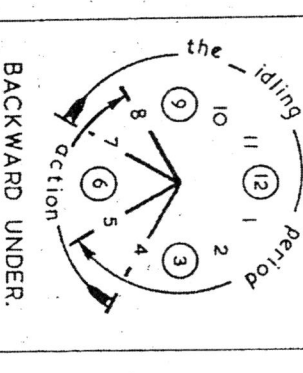

Diagram No. 5
THE FORWARD OVER ACTION.
Continues after the Upward Lift Action until it meets the first action again.

The actions follow in this sequence throughout the complete cycle, the change from one action to the other being instinctive after practice and thus a smooth and continuous pressure will be applied to the pedals. The actual changes take place between 5 and 10 past, 20 and 25 past and 20 minutes to the hour and finally between 10 minutes and 5 minutes to 12 o'clock.

Students in this system of training must retain quite clearly in their minds the knowledge that, when these actions are practised separately the idling period indicated in the diagrams is essentially an idling period with not the slightest suggestion of assisting—or even more important—resisting progress. Thorough practice is essential to attain the riding perfection which can be achieved by following this method of riding the bicycle. This process is the art of pedalling a cycle against the more normal process of just pushing it and, with practice, all the advantages which may be obtained by this method will become evident to the rider, who will be removed from the category of a slogger to that of an artist.

Each action analyzed and the movements in turn outlined show the course for the legs to follow through the idling periods of the other actions and it will be found that the feet are guiding the pedals in their correct course instead of being allowed to be forced by the pedals into a circular path which is wasteful of strength and causes muscular fatigue.

Let us commence with the leg action of the DOWNWARD PRESS ACTION. We find the knee bent at the start of the action and the portion of the leg below the knee substantially in compression with a slight lateral tendency forward. As the stroke develops, compression predominates until past the half-way position, when the lateral tendency returns but this time with a backwards tendency. The thigh commences laterally downward and develops on its way to a state of compression almost completely so at the end of its action.

The BACKWARD UPWARD UNDER ACTION is performed by a backward lateral action of the entire leg but the slight compression for half the distance and the tensioning developed in the remainder of the movement should not be forgotten. The tensioning takes place as the point of extremity is passed.

The next movement, the UPWARD LIFT ACTION, starts with the leg considerably extended and then the lower half of the leg develops a lateral inclination. From this position the lower lift which, when it reacts against the forward kick, tends towards compression of the leg at the end of the action.

The final action, the FORWARD OVER ACTION, which follows the Upward lift begins with the knee bent and the foot having a backward inclination. From this position the lower half of the leg is laterally operated in a forward kick while the thigh lifts for half the distance travelled and presses down for the remainder of the movement thus placing the thigh in compression ready to recommence the Downward press action again.

The arms during all these movements are in a tensed state, pushing and pulling on the handlebars as natural instinct demands.

When all these actions have been practised sufficiently and the rider feels confident that he can combine all the four movements

APPENDIX C

smoothly, he will then be reaching a stage of perfection in riding which will pay full dividends for all the time spent in practice. A fit rider without undue exertion will attain untold power and will at the same time always be able to maintain a reserve of strength, for the CIRCULAR ACTION correctly performed is absolutely the last word in efficient cycle riding.

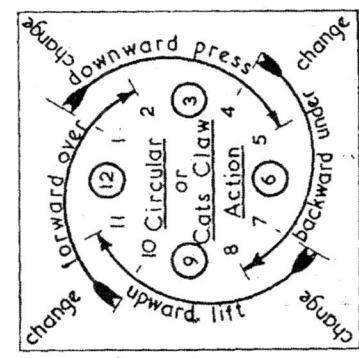

Diagram No. 6

CIRCULAR OR CATS CLAW ACTION

Many an old-time rider has attempted to explain the meaning of sprinting or jumping—some liken it to the act of picking up the cycle and running with it, but it is really a study of really scientific methods of turning the pedals to give the rider really unequalled advantages. To help you to clarify the feeling of correctly performing the CIRCULAR ACTION watch a cat or kitten at play. The kitten will clutch at an object with its front claws and simultaneously push it away with the hind paws, then, bringing them up again in front of itself will again tear away from a point very near to where the object is being clutched. The CIRCULAR ACTION demands similar actions. In the use of this style of pedalling, one will find oneself at one time doing the UPWARD LIFT and at other times the other actions of the complete circular action. During actual racing this practice should be adopted for the act of changing over from one action to the other will be noticed by the opposition and will disconcert them and tend to intimidate them. It should be used as a preparatory measure to applying the fully developed CATS CLAW or CIRCULAR ACTION in a similar manner which a weight lifter adopts prior to actually making the lift.

By switching from one action to the other the muscles will be rested because first one set of muscles are taxed and then a different set as the action changes.

The actions so descibed should be performed naturally and you should train yourself to make the movement instinctive, thus making use of the maximum strength available. Over emphatic ankling may only serve to impair efficiency where the CIRCULAR ACTION, smoothly performed, will definitely give the rider advantage over his opponents.

We have so far dealt only with the sprinter but the full technique may be applied in modified terms to serve all branches of the sport. We cyclists should learn from the sprinter as the designers of record breaking aircraft and motor cars learn to apply the lessons learned to everyday use in the air and in car design.

The short distance road man should imitate as far as possible the sprinter using the CATS CLAW in all its phases except on hills where the THRUSTING ACTION should be used. The UPWARD LIFT ACTION serves one well during rough going as it diverts any foot lagging to the front downward stroke, thus assisting progress instead of retarding it.

Longer distance riders can also benefit by use of the system outlined in this pamphlet, changing from one action to another

to provide rest for the various muscle groups.

The pedalling system in the whole of this leaflet is well suited to be used in conjunction with the JACK KNIFE SYSTEM outlined in my first pamphlet and when the two have been practised and successfully combined, a truer sense of power and perfection in riding the Bicycle will be realised.

Printed by Stewarts of Morden Ltd., 359 Kingston Road, London, S.W. 20.

Leaflet No 3 Price 4d.
Copyright applied for.

We learn by Teaching

PROGRESS of DESIGN

A study of Cycle Construction throughout the past years and reasons for adopting

"THE JACK KNIFE POSITION"

by

FREDERICK H PRATT & SON,
F.I.Cy.C.T.

Complete Cycle Engineers

BRIGHTON ROAD, SALFORDS,
REDHILL - - SURREY
TELEPHONE: HORLEY 1168

agents for

CLAUD BUTLER, RALEIGH INDUSTRIES Etc

A Comprehensive stock of all Cyclists' needs.

PROGRESS OF DESIGN

PREFACE

The purpose of publishing this series of leaflets is not to pronounce dogmatic views about what should, or should not, be correct positioning of oneself on a bicycle, but to make available to everyone the basic scientific facts which always prevail when one is exerting natural energy to propel oneself forward on the simple mechanical construction known to all as a bicycle. We hope also, to show how alteration to the shape of the bicycle affects personal comfort and to demonstrate the advantage, or otherwise, of the changes which have taken place. The reader will then be in a position to mould personal needs to the best advantage, knowing how far he can indulge in favourite habits without loss of power in some other direction.

The development to upright frame design represents the progress of cycle construction during the last twenty years. Until then the public was not angle conscious and unquestioningly accepted what the manufacturer offered. Even in these more enlightened days we find the multitude guided by the few, as the latest fashions are included in design specifications irrespective of whether there is sound reason for their inclusion or not.

Nevertheless these crazes, be they good or bad, must have been provoked by the need for improvement, so to find the reason for them, we must analyse the original state of affairs to find the imperfections which started things moving. It requires boldness to undertake the task of reproducing a picture on so debatable a subject. So we venture, rightly or wrongly, to present to the reader what we believe to be the true facts which outline the gradual change in design and to challenge the good sense of results.

Fifteen or twenty years ago, sixty-eight and sixty-six degrees head and seat angles were commonplace, slants of sixty-three and even sixty being nothing unusual. These machines were provided with nearly straight forks, they had no triangles approaching twenty inches in length (centre to centre) bottom brackets around eleven and twelve inches high, the standard crank length was then seven inches, but could frequently be found as much as one and a half inches longer, while wheelbases measured in the region of forty-two and a half to forty-four and a half inches. The rider was sitting pretty well back, the pedals placed well forward in relation to the peak of the saddle, handlebars reasonably convenient, but the front wheel was lightly loaded and stuck well forward in advance of the rest of the outfit. This undesirable distribution

APPENDIX C

of weight caused a high centre of gravity to occur over the rear of the machine; this condition being aggravated by the excessive height of the bottom brackets thus pushing the weight still higher. Somewhere between this rearward high weight and the contact with the ground a fulcrum occurred, causing a considerable sideways movement, or wag; reacting from every movement of the rider's body, this being multiplied through the length of the machine with the greatest affect influencing the front wheel. The almost straight fork obviously possessed too little offset to avoid fall and rise of the head when turned; the falling weight of the body forcing the turn caused very tricky steering necessitating arm work to lift this weight again, on bringing the machine back to a straight course. These were the conditions which furnished the primary need for improvement.

The first change to recall was the introduction of curved seat pins and swan neck handlebar stems. This certainly brought the high centre of gravity forward, so distributing the weight of the body more equally between the two wheels, but steering conditions were still very bad due to the increased force to the turn being added by the more forward weight.

At this juncture a little technical data about steering angles will assist a clearer understanding. Each head angle demands a certain fork offset to avoid rise and fall of the head when steering. A line drawn through the centre of the head and extended well down below the fork crown and another drawn parallel to it, but this time passing through the centre of the front wheel spindle, indicates the fork offset by the shortest distance between the two lines.

Diagram No. 1 shows a simple method of arriving at the correct amount of fork offset for any given head angle together with any size wheel. The layman must accept this as a fact and it is easy to understand and quickly arrived at by a simple demonstration on the drawing-board; anyone who is a good enough mathematician can prove the method by calculation. In the calculation head angle, speed, degrees of leaning must all be considered, also the point at which the tyre touches the ground as this contact moves to another point further round the wheel in the process of turning. First draw a line to represent the ground, next draw a circle touching this line representing the wheel (this circle may be drawn to scale). Now draw a line perpendicular to the ground passing through the wheel centre, and finally draw a third line at the desired head angle and cutting the perpendicular at the wheel centre. Now bisect the angle formed between the perpendicular and the head angle: the correct fork offset is represented by the distance between the point at which the bisecting line cuts the wheel radius line and the point of contact of the wheel with the ground.

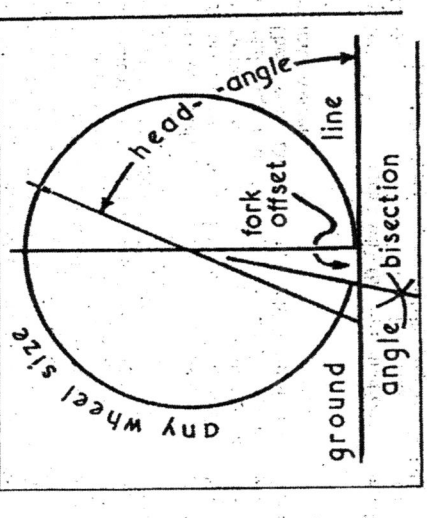

Too much offset causes rise and fall of the front of the machine and too little causes fall and rise when steering. The weight of the body in the first instance forces the machine in a straight line, while the second condition results in very sensitive steering because the weight of the body assists the turn. Our advice on this is to specify the correct offset for any given head angle, but to exceed this slightly is a good fault as this tends to add stability on a straight course. The angle conscious period which started next, developed from semi-upright designs increasing in steepness as time progressed. By this process the steering considerably improved; as more upright head angles demand less fork offset to avoid rise and fall, the combination became nearer right, perfection being acquired in some cases. The craze for short wheel bases has, however, always persisted, and has proved to be perhaps the worst enemy of all as its intervention usually spoiled any good results otherwise gained. Owners, on discovering a space between the rear wheel and the more upright seat tube, immediately took steps to shorten the rear triangle, to bring the wheel close up again and so created a brand new undesirable high centre of gravity over the rear of the machine.

It is possible to give endless examples similar to this; some absurd in the extreme. We find weird arrangements substituting seat tubes in many instances on shortened rear triangles.

The most recent demand for very low bottom brackets is with the object of lowering the centre of gravity without lengthening the wheel base. The idea is sound, but results only in making the best of a bad job, as this lengthens the down tube. These remarks suggest that for the most part the changes made during this past

APPENDIX C

period have had little advantage, but actions speak louder than words as we must realise when we consider the time improvements achieved in every kind of race.

Human beings can readily accommodate themselves to adverse conditions, and quite often in an undertaking can attain better results from their labour if they merely think a new condition is to their advantage. Also changes made gradually over a long period can reach extreme proportions without the individual even noticing them; the gradual process in effect educates and moulds them to the new ideas which are not necessarily to the best. It is possible for the rider to change to a completely new frame, the design of which will immediately appear to be suitable for him. He will feel comfortable and will be so impressed by the improvement in steering, or some other condition, that he may not notice personal discomfort resulting from too much weight being placed on his arms or a strained position of head and neck. Disregarding these troubles and, with the enthusiasm common to all cyclists, he goes blithely ahead and may well, with his new found control, do extremely well in competitions in spite of the personal discomfort referred to above.

A good bike is like a good bed. Many a person will boast that they can sleep on a clothes line but common sense suggests that they would sleep much more restfully, and with much more beneficial sleep, in a comfortable bed. So a cyclist can achieve his ambition more comfortably and effectively on a well designed bicycle.

The next paragraphs explain what happens when a change to a new frame is made. Let us consider what happens if a rider, with his body supposed to be frozen into one particular riding position, is made to take up a new position relative to his cycle frame. If he is made to rotate forward about the bottom bracket then the weight is gradually transferred from the saddle to the handlebars, but, if he is moved back to give a more slanting angle, then, the reverse action takes place and the weight is gradually transferred to the saddle. The following details will explain the process more clearly. A straight line radiating from the centre of a circle radius 22in. and a second radiating from the same centre and finishing on the circumference of the circle but ⅜in. to one side of the first line (measured along the arc) will be found to contain an angle between the two lines of approximately 1° so, by working off a 22in. frame size, we find that on moving the top of the seat tube (where the saddle pin goes in) each ⅜in. moved through is equivalent to altering the slope by 1°. This means that the position becomes more upright by forward movement and in the reverse direction less upright by similar deduction. This provides a good guide to the number of degrees involved when seat tube slants are altered. Each ⅜in. of movement represents one of 360 degrees of a complete circle with the bottom bracket as centre.

The point where the hands grip the handlebar is the next consideration. This point is always more than 22in. from the bottom bracket centre, so although the rotation radiates from the bottom bracket centre, so although the rotation radiates from the bottom axis, the distance travelled through in moving through 1° is more than ⅜in. radius. A particular point of note is also that the locality of this movement is appreciably horizontally opposed to the axis, and therefore the direction of travel is such that if the seat is made more upright then the position of the grip is lowered whereas if the seat is made more upright then the grip is, relatively higher.

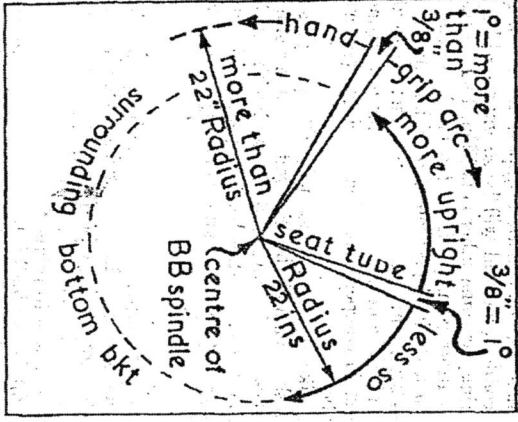

This diagram clearly shows how any rider's position can be rotated about the bracket centre, changing the aspect of the rider only in relation to the ground and the force of gravity (which is the effect of the weight of his body).

Next let us consider the conduct of the proud possessor of a new SUPER ULTRA-MODERN UPRIGHT lightweight. He first decides that the top tube is somewhat short and changes the extension for one considerably longer; after another try-out he decides that if the bars were lower his problem would be settled but finds that the head is too high to allow of further lowering. (Expander bolt headfittings have returned to favour because they are small and allow the handlebar stem to be pushed in lower than head clip types). At this stage many readers resort to sliding type extensions with the sliding clip under the extension tube; others

APPENDIX C

In the earliest designs referred to herein, the rider assumed a posture similar to our "JACK KNIFE" position; he was seated well behind the bottom bracket with the handlebars relatively lower than the modern upright mounts. This quite effectively closed the angle between push and pull of the legs and arms. The fault was in the layout of the machine. Loss of front wheel command was the first complaint. The forward position of this wheel gave the feeling that it was separated from the rest of the machine and matters were made worse by the bad steering combination of fork offset and head angle which gave the impression that the front wheel lay on its side when a turn was made. The procedure of setting head and seat tubes to more upright angles gained advantage on this score, we agree, but it failed on the other hand by opening the vital angle between push and pull and creating at the same time a far-back pedalling position as explained above.

The unwise desire for short rear triangles brought the rear wheel forward and in effect the rider's weight came over the back of the machine once more, thus causing back wheel wag and the need for ample front wheel toe clearance to permit control of the resultant wobble.

Now let us return to a consideration of the early design of 68° or less, head and seat tubes parallel, together with bad steering facilities and misplaced weight distribution where the rider was accommodated more or less comfortably but at the expense of control. To acquire the "JACK KNIFE" arrangement from this basic design demands that the head be set up to a semi-upright angle. This would be around 71° with a fork offset of 2¼in. effecting a shortening of the front centres between wheel spindle and bottom bracket axle and correcting the steering fault at the same time. This done further shortening of this measurement would be accomplished by the use of shorter top and down tubes so bringing the head and fork assembly back closer to the rider but essentially keeping it at the same angle, in this case 71° of course.

Small people cannot depart from parallel angles otherwise a too small head and a too long top tube results, a compromise being necessary between suitable frame angles and fork offset. Smaller wheels however permit of proper design in proportion.

To maintain arm reach and clearance between knees and handlebars with adequately shortened front centres extensions to the handlebars can be employed where necessary. These have the advantage of enhancing front wheel control by the more forward handlebar position they produce. Wide bars allow room for the knees to pass between the arms and allow for chest expansion. Decisions should always be arrived at by conservative measures. There is a distinct line between being too far forward, causing the angle between push and pull to be unnecessarily opened, and, on the other hand being too far back so loosing command of the front have special stems made with the extension bent downwards like a chicken's neck with no bone in it. After all this there still seems to be something left to be desired but nothing more can be done except for the rider to adapt himself to the remaining inadequacies

Upright angles rotate the rider's position forward, this new saddle position does not cause discomfort to the rider, as the seat tube still assumes the same relation to the thrust of the legs but, as explained, the hand grip is moved substantially in a downward direction and soon meets the fixed point where the head fittings prevent further movement. To maintain arm reach, therefore, there is no alternative but to push the bar forward by means of an extension. This opens up the angle between the power pull of the arms and the push of the legs which detracts from efficient use of available strength. The weight of the body is diverted from the legs to the arms by the force of gravity and the rider to have clear vision. sarily be strained back to allow the rider to have clear vision.

A machine which answers to the description of a MASS START MODEL in general has a very upright head, a big sweeping fork-rake, the offset being around 3 to 3¼ inches. This produces a long front centre measurement allowing plenty of front wheel toe clearance. The seat tube angle is usually less upright than the head, but the shortness of the rear triangle, and the steepness still existing in the seat tube creates a relatively far-back pedalling position. The big fork offset causes a lot of rise and fall to the front of the machine when turned. The weight of the rider is forcing the cycle in a straight line, this tends to cause corners to be taken wide the bars needing to be held round against the weight of the rider. Our continental friends take full advantage of the stability so produced and on a straight course they are able to leave the saddle and climb over the front of the machine (closing the angle between push and pull in so doing) and "dance" up the hill, as they term this method. Since the machine needs little control they can thrash themselves, and their machines, unmercifully, without fear of upset.

The opposite to these methods is the "JACK KNIFE" position which, like closing a jack knife reduces the angle between power pull of the arms and push of the legs without leaving the saddle. The rider's position in this case is rotated backwards about the centre of the bottom bracket and, because of the upward moving direction of the new position of the hand grip, the head can be held naturally and unstrained while the handlebar can remain where it is and be in a relatively lower position than it was before. On completion of the desired alteration the handlebar may be brought back closer to the rider's body until the vital angle is closed to a minimum.

Only the "JACK KNIFE" design as outlined in our leaflet No. 1 adequately lends itself to this posture.

APPENDIX C

wheel. Our advice is, to indulge freely in setting the seat position as far back as possible without losing command of the front wheel. When the rider is assuming a too far back saddle position he will experience a very heavy pressure on the saddle and on a long journey will suffer saddle soreness. Better advantage can be taken of a far back saddle position when a rider is fresh as he has more live weight on the pedals and less on the saddle. As fatigue overtakes him a more relaxed condition takes control with the result that he sits more heavily on the saddle.

We now draw your attention to Diagram No. 3, its purpose being to represent the title of this publication, viz., "PROGRESS OF DESIGN." Broadly speaking this design is the outcome of years of follow-my-leader developments but the diagram is intended to emphasise the things which, in our humble opinion, should be avoided. Finally we come to Diagram No. 4 which reflects in its make-up the "JACK KNIFE POSITION."

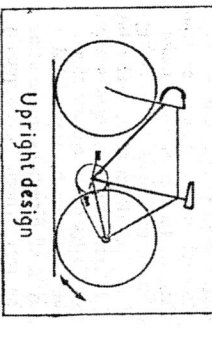

Diagram No. 3

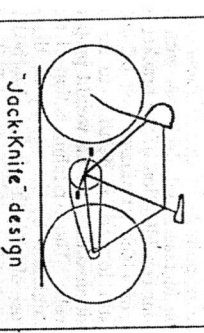

Diagram No. 4

In Diagram No. 3 we find upright angles and shallow fork rake producing an almost innovably rigid head assembly. There is also a long and thereby very whippy down head tube which is accentuated by having the lowest possible bottom bracket and long front centre measurement. This, and the upright seat, all contribute to a far back pedalling position. To complete the picture we have a short rear triangle transmitting the resultant bottom bracket pendulum action directly to the rear wheel causing this to wag about from side to side (as indicated by the double-headed arrow). Terrific loss of power results due to the friction between tyre and ground. This sideways wag is generated from the top of the down tube where it joins the head, being held taut at this point by the rigidity of the head assembly. The swing of the bracket (pendulum action) bends the tube from side to side subjecting it to undue strain and frequently causes fracture by fatigue at a point about an inch or so from the actual joint. Many manufacturers have replaced these broken tubes free of charge under guarantee. As they can find no evidence of damage by accident they blame faulty materials or workmanship when, in fact, the fault lies in the design of the frame. This design is usually developed to meet the customer's own request, so that subject to him having refused the manufacturer's advice, the onus for the breakage is really the customer's. A too straight fork makes a rigid head at any angle and tends to cause this breakage. Tandems are particularly vulnerable in this respect.

Diagram No. 4 shows us another picture and is best appreciated by surveying it in the reverse order to Diagram No. 3. The rear wheel is held by the rigid, although unusually long, rear triangle as all the tubes comprising it are in tension or compression, the construction being triangulated in all directions. Continuing forward from the bracket we find a short down tube, preferably of large diameter, meeting a head of semi-upright steepness which in turn possesses a fork with flexible blades of the correct offset. The advantage of short top and down tubes can be appreciated in the same way as the structure supporting the rear wheel. Consequently the lateral rigidity of this half of the frame depends upon the stiffness of each individual tube, these frame members being in tension or compression only through the longitudinal axis of the machine. The magnitude of this stiffness increases as the diameter of the tube increases but decreases with increase in length. Returning to our consideration of the bracket we find a sloping seat tube, the top of which terminates well behind the bracket centre, but which is still forward in relation to the rear wheel spindle. A rider positioned thus has his weight properly distributed between the two wheels. The pendulum action of the bottom bracket is reduced to a minimum by the rigidity of the short stiff down tube, the side thrust of pedalling being absorbed by the fork resilience. Laterally rigid fork blades such as "D" to round section convert lateral flexion to the longitudinal axis. Spring through the length of the machine is largely recovered by the rebound but the sideways whip is a complete loss as this results only in frictional loss between tyre and road.

The short distance between front centres, that is the distance between spindle and bracket axle, insures command of the front wheel as explained. Front wheel clearance can be improved by the

APPENDIX C

use of side grip toe clips instead of the usual type which pass over the front of the toe. This is not a new idea but we have a toe clip in the process of development which is novel in design and which is proving excellent in use. The danger, should the toe catch the **front wheel**, is lessened **because the rider's toe is not a fixed object** to the same extent as with a metal toe clip and does not offer the same resistance on contact. The risk of damage to the toe clip when it is swinging out of use is entirely eliminated as it is too short to touch the ground. Subject to the popularity of this idea, we intend to interest a reputable firm with a view to manufacturing these in quantity as this project is too ambitious an undertaking for ourselves in this early stage of our career.

The suggested danger resulting from the toe catching the front wheel or mudguard is in fact almost non-existent when using properly proportioned Jack Knife design. At speeds over eight miles per hour it is impossible to touch and, at speeds lower than this it is a simple matter, after a little practice to nip round in between periods when the crank is in the position where the toe is unlikely to touch. Remember that bounce control improves with speed, your safety lies in speed.

We sincerely hope that cyclists in general will benefit from our efforts to enlighten them on this hitherto little known subject of the theory of design. Those who do not agree with us in principle will no doubt gain food for thought.

APPENDIX C

Leaflet No. 4

Copyright applied for.

Price 6d.

We learn by Teaching

POSITIONING
WITH A PURPOSE

A study showing diagrammatical stages of how to accommodate oneself to

"THE JACK KNIFE POSITION"

by

FREDERICK H. PRATT & SON,
F.I.Cy.E.T.

Complete Cycle Engineers

BRIGHTON ROAD, SALFORDS,
SURREY.

TELEPHONE HORLEY 1165

agents for

CLAUD BUTLER, RALEIGH INDUSTRIES, Etc.

———

A Comprehensive stock of all Cyclists' needs.

POSITIONING
WITH A PURPOSE

by
FREDERICK H. PRATT

The publication of this leaflet, in continuation of my third one entitled PROGRESS OF DESIGN, is made with the object of illustrating practically the theoretical deductions which were made in the previous pamphlet and to show how to apply the JACK KNIFE design suitably to the individual rider.

The diagrams in this pamphlet are not strictly true to scale as the measurements are based upon the approximate calculation three-eighths of an inch equalling the movement through 1 degree round an arc of a circle of 22in. radius so that, should the drawings be scaled up, a discrepancy will be discovered. This discrepancy will be particularly noticeable between diagrams 1 and 4 because the inaccuracy due to the approximation is multiplied through all the four diagrams. This does not, however, detract from my purpose of guiding interested cyclists along the right lines, leaving them to work out for themselves the exact measurement after gaining correct knowledge of the principles involved. I must assume that the reader accepts the JACK KNIFE position for what it is worth and, after reading this leaflet and noting the substance of the drawings, he should then be quite sure of his opinion about the good sense, or otherwise, of JACK KNIFE versus UPRIGHT frame design.

I now ask the reader to study diagram No. 1 carefully as the names of the component members of a bicycle frame are given and it shows how the dimensions apply. The terms shown in this diagram will be used throughout this leaflet and I hope that they will help the reader to understand more clearly the ensuing pages of the story of "Positioning with a Purpose."

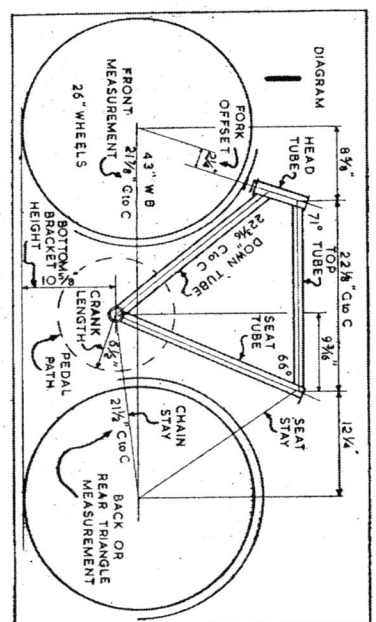

DIAGRAM 1

APPENDIX C

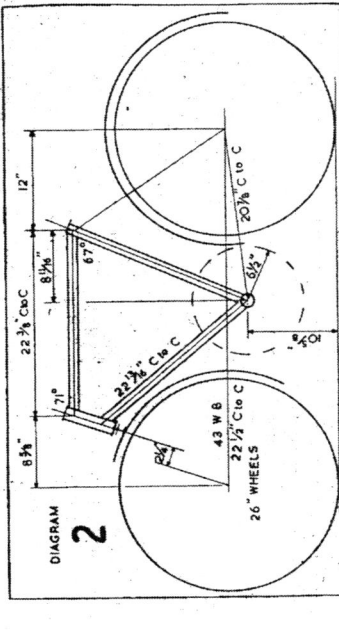
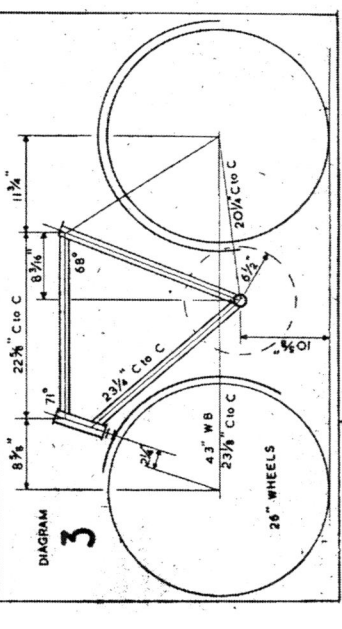
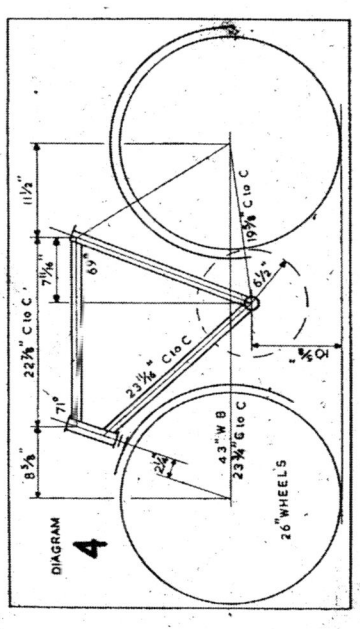

Abbreviations used in this leaflet:—

C to C is an abbreviation for centre to centre.

On the top tube this measurement applies to its length between the centres of the head and seat tubes.

On the down tube it applies to its length, measuring between the centre of the head tube and the centre of the bottom bracket.

The front centre to centre measurement indicates the shortest distance between the centre of the front wheel spindle and the bottom bracket axle.

The back or rear triangle measurement gives the distance between the centre of the bottom bracket axle and the rear wheel spindle.

W.B. indicates the wheel base and is measured in a straight line from the centre of the front to the centre of the rear wheel spindles.

The bottom bracket height is quite obvious; it indicates the height of the bracket from the ground. This will be abbreviated to B.B. height.

The crank length is the measurment from the centre of the bottom bracket spindle and the centre of the pedal spindle.

The dotted line circle surrounding the B.B. assembly is the path of the pedals when the cranks are rotated.

The fork offset shows how much the fork blade curves away from the head tube centre to the fork end where the front wheel spindle is held.

Diagrams 1, 2, 3 and 4 represent the JACK KNIFE design as truly intended. Diagram 1 is a severe application in respect of the toes overlapping the front wheel, whilst in diagrams 2 and 3 this condition is gradually moderated until in diagram 4 we find a front measurement allowing ample clearance between toe and mudguard when the wheel is turned. A clear picture of the difference between one and another is evident in the diagrams if the reader studies the position of the B.B. assembly from one diagram to the next. The circle indicating the pedal path can be seen to be nearest to the front wheel in diagram 1 moving gradually towards the rear wheel from diagram 1 to diagram 4.

All four diagrams feature a 71 degree head angle and fork offset of 2$\frac{1}{4}$ins. This head angle provides the desirable semi-upright position with which to avoid rise and fall and demands a fork offset which is pliable but not too spongy in use so giving ideal conditions for bounce control. A more fitting description of this action is "riding the front wheel," as explained in leaflet No. 1.

Positioning a rider comfortably (disregarding for the moment the question of greatest advantage) involves two dimensions only, one being the angle or slope of the seat tube and the second the length of the top tube. The remainder of the design can be varied at will without affecting the posture of the rider. The head can assume any angle in combination with any offset fork. Front wheel toe clearance can be large or small whilst the B.B. can be high or low and the rear triangle long or short. It is important to note the way in which a new combination of these two dimensions affects the rest of the frame layout and therefore in my analysis of these diagrams the top tube length and the seat tube angle will provide the key to the theories expounded in the following paragraphs. These theories follow careful investigation, over a period of years, of the possibilities of improvement in cycle design.

As previously mentioned, the head angle and fork offset remain the same on all four diagrams and it will be found that the wheel base and B.B. height also remain constant so that the effect on altering the top tube length and seat angle can be readily appreciated in relation to these three fixed dimensions. In diagram 1 there is a top tube length of 22$\frac{1}{8}$ins. and a seat tube sloping at 66 degrees to the ground. Diagram 2 shows a combination of 22$\frac{3}{8}$ins. C to C top tube and 67 deg. seat angle. Diagram 3 provides a top tube a quarter of an inch longer still and a seat tube angle another degree more upright. The same increase occurs on diagram 4 bringing the top tube measurement up to 22$\frac{7}{8}$ins. and seat angle up to 69 deg. The change from diagram 1 to diagram 2 is in the same proportion as that from diagram 2 to diagram 3 and there is the same proportionate change from 3 to 4. The difference between diagrams 1 and 4 therefore amounts to an increase of $\frac{3}{4}$in. to the top tube length and a seat tube 3 deg. more upright.

Bearing these basic differences in mind, attention should now be devoted to the effect which these changes have in relation to the fixed measurements, namely, the wheel base, B.B. height, head angle and fork offset. The first, and perhaps the most important consideration to the reader is the front C to C measurement with regard to toe clearance. It will be found that the increase from one diagram to the next is $\frac{5}{8}$in., giving a difference of 1$\frac{7}{8}$in. between diagrams 1 and 4. Next note the measurement of the rear triangle. This you will find decreases by an equal amount, that is, it is $\frac{5}{8}$in. shorter from one diagram to the next and after three changes will have decreased by three times this amount. The process of these changes should be regarded in the following manner: from one diagram to the next the seat tube has been rotated about the B.B. centre in a forward direction through 1 deg. amounting to approximately $\frac{3}{8}$in. movement at the top of the tube. This in effect shortens the top tube by $\frac{3}{8}$in. but so far the front C to C is unaltered. From this new position the seat tube (throughout its entire length) moves bodily backwards a distance of $\frac{5}{8}$in. so affecting a lengthening of the top tube to $\frac{1}{4}$in. more than its original measurement and the front C to C measurement increases $\frac{5}{8}$in. to full amount of the movement. This explanation, together with study of the diagrams, show the result of the changes clearly. After appreciating this let us then devote our attention to the remaining dimensions, so far unmentioned.

The B.B. height is dimension No. 1. This does not alter but merely moves back in a horizontal direction through the changes but, because of this movement, the rear triangle (dimension No. 2) is accordingly shortened. The wheel base being a fixed measurement provided the cause of this as any increase in the front C to C measurement automatically reduces the back by an equal amount.

The top end of the seat tube in relation to the vertical line drawn down to the B.B. centre is dimension No. 3. It commences in diagram 1 by measuring 9 3/16in. and gradually decreases as the seat is set more uprightly. Moving to the other end of the top tube to where this joins the centre of the head tube, another static measurement is to be found. This is dimension No. 4 and measures the distance from this point to a vertical line drawn down to the front wheel centre. This measurement is constant because of the unchanging head angle and fork offset. Dimension No. 5 is at the first mentioned end of the top tube where it meets the top end of the seat tube and indicates the distance from this point to a vertical line drawn down to the rear wheel spindle. This measurement, it will be found, decreases from one diagram to the next at the same rate as the measurement of the top tube lengthens. The last dimension, No. 6, is the down tube C to C measurement, and in my view, this measurement is of vital importance.

Diagram No. 1 shows a down tube 22 3/16in. long from C to C. In diagram No. 2 C to C dimension is 22 13/16in., in diagram 3, 23$\frac{1}{4}$in., and in diagram 4 it is 23 11/16in. That is, a difference of approximately $\frac{1}{2}$in. from one diagram to the next and of 1$\frac{1}{2}$in. between diagrams 1 and 4. This is a consideration indeed as this increases the magnitude of B.B. pendulum action, as was explained in my leaflet No. 3.

Leaving the technical side of the question for the moment, let us now view the situation from the rider's point of view. He is finding with this forward rotation of the seat tube and the gradual lengthening of the top tube that the pedalling position is becoming pushed back and that his saddle is gradually assuming a position further and further away from the handlebars. Also the angle between the power pull of the arms and push of the legs is widening. The rider is thereby losing some advantage of his strength

APPENDIX C

and, at the same time, is lessening his command of the front wheel by the removal of some of his weight from it. His weight is in fact (because it is further back) tending towards the creation of a rearward high centre of gravity. Last, but not least, the influence of the thrusts of pedalling is accordingly being transferred from the front wheel to the rear. In other words the blade of the jack knife is opening. This summary of the first four diagrams shows how the rider on the one hand is robbed of some advantage at the expense of acquiring front wheel toe clearance. The importance of one advantage outweighing the advantage of the other must be left to the judgment of the individual.

If a machine is intended strictly for racing, and the object is to obtain maximum advantage of available strength, then the rider is well advised to learn to tolerate toe overlap. Perseverance in this soon produces dividends as it is easily tolerated when a machine is correctly designed. If, on the other hand, the rider's intention is purely for pleasure, then a little more toe clearance may assure peace of mind, but good advice here is to allow just sufficient toe clearance and no more.

Diagram 3 represents our recommendation for this purpose as this provides a front C to C of sufficient length, not to guarantee that the toe will miss, but to remove the element of danger should the rider fear that this exists. The toe will still be likely to touch but not to cause inconvenience.

All of these first four diagrams represent my recommendations, all are based upon sound ideas and they are a moderate interpretation of my ideas and are ordinary bicycles which may be considered as our future standard productions and will be supplied to requests stating the diagram number desired.

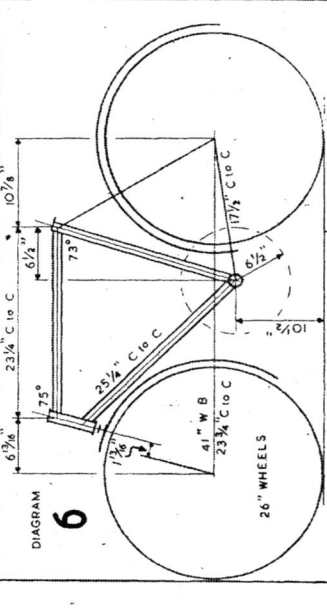

Our attention can now pass on to diagrams 5 and 6. The object of these is to attempt to apply JACK KNIFE principles to more upright frame angles. This should help those who believe in the JACK KNIFE system of riding, but feel dubious of upsetting their present style, with which they are already achieving success.

The JACK KNIFE position IS different. A different muscle group from that used on upright machines is called upon. The forward pedalling position demands a true pedalling action as the legs and, in particular, the thighs, require lifting much more. The CAT'S CLAW action of pedalling as described in our leaflet No. 2, "PEDALLING A BICYCLE EFFICIENTLY," can be appreciated immediately on consideration of a less upright seat angle. The upright over the bracket saddle position in contrast demands a backward treading and upward dragging action. The JACK KNIFE position together with the CAT'S CLAW action utilises the strength of the arms to assist the power of the legs, whilst an exaggeratedly upright seat angle allows the legs only to propel the machine forward, as any attempt to pull on the handlebars can only serve to remove the rider from his saddle. In applying JACK KNIFE principles to more upright angles it is our object to provide a stepping stone for the cautious man and to reduce the sudden change from one method to the other. This will enable those whose muscles have been developed on an upright machine to try out the JACK KNIFE method without unduly losing the advantage of their present accumulation of strength by the abrupt switchover from one muscle group to another.

In respect of the following features, diagrams 5 and 6 have the same relationship to one another as have diagrams 2 and 4:

(1) The top tube C to C of diagram 6 is ¾in. longer than that of diagram 5.
(2) The front C to C measurement is 1¼in. more.
(3) The rear triangle is 1¼in. less, whilst the seat tube is 2 deg. more upright.

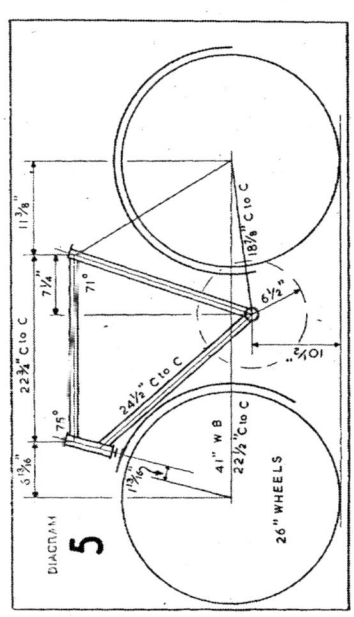

APPENDIX C

It will be found also that the head angle, fork offset, wheel base, crank length and B.B. height remain constant. This new set of more upright dimensions must indicate a further departure from our original agreed ideal portrayed by diagram No. 1. Before drawing comparisons between diagrams 2 and 5, which is our intention, let us again refer to diagram 1. It is agreed that this possesses the most suitable head and fork offset combination, and we may add that the front C to C, for all intents and purposes, is the shortest practicable, whilst the angle between the power pull of the arms and push of the legs is closed to a desirable minimum.

From this state of practical perfection we move our attention back to diagram 2 again. This must be considered as the first stage of modification, or the commencement of the departure from JACK KNIFE principles. To continue our comparison, we find that in diagram 5 the head and seat tubes are 4 deg. more upright than in diagram 2. This represents a further and considerable departure from our first agreed standard of perfection but our object is to compromise, so this must be accepted, remembering that the cost of this compromise is measured by the degree of efficiency and comfort gained from it. Other results of this change are that the new head angle demands less fork offset to avoid rise and fall of the machine when steering (as explained in leaflet No. 3), this less flexible fork reduces the bounce control, the down and top tubes have to be lengthened in order to maintain the same front C to C measurement. This in turn aggravates the B.B. pendulum action with still further deterioration to the JACK KNIFE condition. The wheel bases on these specimens are shorter than in diagrams 1, 2, 3 and 4, being the more usually accepted dimensions of present day standards. This is agreeable to some extent because of the more forward position of the rider. It will be noticed that the measurement from the centre of the head to the vertical line drawn down to the front wheel centre is less than on diagram 2 and it will also be found that the measurement from the centre of the seat tube to the rear wheel centre is less. The rider's weight is more or less correctly distributed between the two wheels in both designs. The 10½in. B.B. height has little effect on the general plan, serving only to lower the centre of gravity slightly at the expense of a relatively longer down tube. A 22½in. front C to C measurement is the shortest practicable when planning along these lines and quite a lot of pendulum action occurs as a result of reduced bounce control, so adding to the danger of front wheel toe overlap. This arrangement which features a shallower fork offset, lengthened down tube and short rear triangle could be improved in principle by increasing the fork offset to 2¼in. this would recover fork flexibility and shorten the top and down tubes enhancing bounce control. The stability of the machine would improve because the resulting rise and fall of the machine would tend to force the machine upon a straight course, and the shorter down tube would reduce the magnitude of B.B. pendulum action.

Both diagrams 5 and 6 would benefit by this alteration and a further advantage would result by lengthening the rear triangles, particularly in the instance of diagram 6. This would move the rear wheel away from the influence of pedalling thrust and position the rider relatively more forward on the machine. These alterations are, in effect, a process of recovering the JACK KNIFE principles.

The remaining part of this leaflet will be criticisms of various riding styles and my observation of the experiments personally carried out in my efforts to demonstrate the merits of some of these methods. In venturing an opinion of the variations accepted as general riding, habits I contend that all are graduations removed from the JACK KNIFE position as outlined in this series of leaflets towards the principles of upright angles and short rear triangles, or the tendency to otherwise remove the rider's weight backward over the rear wheel. To arrive at a satisfactory conclusion about the merits of a particular riding character, my policy has been to exaggerate the main features of the style with the object of bringing out the value prominently. It is with this in mind that I include diagrams 7 and 8 in my illustrations.

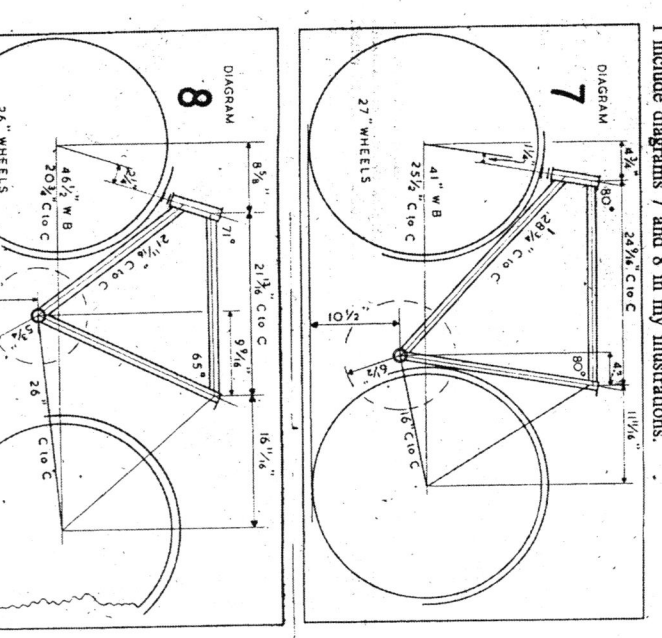

APPENDIX C

In diagram 7 will be found an exaggerated version of upright design, and in diagram 8 the features, also unnecessarily exaggerated, are of the JACK KNIFE position.

Recalling experiences of past years I must necessarily deal first with the experiences of myself as the person concerned with the first part of our trading name, Frederick H. Pratt, and later introduced the second part, " and Son," otherwise, Philip Noel Pratt, from the time when this young enthusiast reached the age where he became capable of taking part in the exploits.

In 1918 I was a schoolboy and had just got beyond the stage of borrowing my sister's bicycle and had become the proud owner of a new company-built machine. It was an example of the rigid back type of frame having solidly brazed seat stays which were just then replacing the bolted up type of seat assembly now found only in full roadster machines. The machine was small, the front C to C measurement allowed sufficient toe clearance to avoid catching the front wheel, and the rear triangle was short. This latter statement is confirmed by a friend who had an identical model, for he says that he used to boast that there was no room for a box of kippers to be carried between the seat tube and the rear tyre. The angles must have been around 70 deg. head and seat tubes parallel. This is, of course, guesswork, not actual measurement, for no cyclist was angle conscious in those days. Needless to say, my new mount and I did not take kindly to each other and I found, for a reason then unknown, that my club mates usually dropped me during "tear ups" and I invariably came home feeling very tired.

Next time that I was able to purchase a bicycle it was the product of a lightweight specialist. The angles of this new mount were approximately 68 deg, seat and head tube parallel, the wheel base was between 42¼in. and 43in. featuring a front C to C measurement of about 24¼in. and rear triangle of around 18½in. These measurements are also based on memory coupled with my years of experience. This machine told a very different story, and when on it I showed many cyclist my back wheel, and when at Herne Hill track I was once told by an ex-world champion that, whilst possessing such a power to sprint as I had just shown, I need never bother to work for a living. Fate, however, had decided that this was not to be, and domestic and business affairs decreed that my life was to be one of hard work and limited cycling. It was with regret that I watched others, who had once been easy prey to me, go forward and become champions in my stead.

Not long after this I was privileged to enter the cycle trade and, although still restricted from taking an active part in cycling as a sport, found a wealth of interest in providing for others. Progress was fast but outwardly uneventful until the six days' bicycle race which was held in the early 1930's, and for which I was privileged to design and make some of the machines used in the race.

One of these, at the rider's own request, was built at 75 deg, head and seat tubes parallel, a 12in. B.B. height was also specified, a 1in. fork offset and a rear triangle C to C as short as possible, leaving no space between the rear tyre and seat tube. This rider lasted less than two days, during which period he had increasingly frequent spills until near the end of his stay less than half an hour lapsed between each fall. During the remaining period of this race I had the opportunity to investigate the designs of the machines of the surviving riders and checked the dimensions of each machine carefully. This knowledge added fresh interest to the last stages of the race for I was now able to watch the riders knowing the differences between their frame designs, and was able to note the reactions of each as the riders performed their tactics.

From this time on, things happened in quick succession, and I found myself involved in catering first for record attempts, then for ordinary road and track races, tandems and pace following events, and at the same time satisfying the needs of club folk, tandem riders, campers, tricyclists and polo players. I was able to take an active part in the game of polo and so learnt much about this entirely different aspect of our sport although in the first-named categories I had, for the most part, to be content to learn by watching and helping others. Naturally, we can only touch vaguely upon these matters as I was not then my own master, but I am now very grateful for the opportunities then presented and which would not otherwise have been available.

Manufacturers, as a whole, adopt a policy of meeting the public demand and so whatever craze is predominating at any particular time they mould their current production (into this style). My son and I, as a firm, feel that there is greater purpose for us than just to follow this policy. All subjects appertaining to cycling which have been mentioned above, will be dealt with gradually through the medium of our leaflets and, as in the past, our reasons for making them will be applied to all our statements and our recommendations.

With favourable fortune, Philip Noel may, all in good time, be able to prove the integrity of these statements. He may, in fact, fulfil his Dad's ambitions! I do not pretend to know all about everything, but few others have as good experience to give them insight into the cyclist's requirements. Certainly, few others can have studied the subject more thoroughly. Having, by the time war broke out, gained much experience. I possessed very definite ideas about good and bad cycle design. Early in 1940, before war conditions got really bad. I evolved and produced for my personal use a machine of the following dimensions: 68 deg. head angle, 24¼in. fork offset, 65 deg. seat tube, 22in. front C to C measurement, 21¼in. top tube. 10½in. R.B. height. 26in. wheels and a 26in. C to C rear triangle. This machine caused much amusement and criticism and suffered many belittling remarks but my mind was made up and I would not be deterred. This machine was ridden throughout,

67

APPENDIX C

and after, the war years and gave much pleasure and satisfaction and was to be the acid test of my recently introduced JACK KNIFE position. The machine was found to be very comfortable to ride and very responsive. The construction was of lugless bronze welded joints. The strain of passing war years, together with the fact that I had now passed the bloom of youth, put me in a rather different category of cyclists from that of previous years and the faster racing class of cyclist frequently proved my master although, quite often, I could give a good account of myself. However, the idea was not to show how good I was but to prove the worth of my now cherished ideas.

Sometimes when out riding, or possibly homeward bound after a day's work, a younger cyclist would come flashing by on a super upright racer, and dash on towards some approaching hill. He would look round in passing and then crouch forward and dash on towards the hill on which he would resort to leaving the saddle and start dancing from side to side on each down stroke of the pedals. I was always ready to accept a challenge of this sort, and with the well-practised cat's claw action of pedalling would increase speed to the foot of the hill and then with the THRUSTING ACTION for the first portion of the climb catch up the challenger. Changing then to either the UPWARD LIFT or else back to the CAT'S CLAW action I would pass the rider who would nearly fall off his machine with surprise fondly thinking that I had been left behind at least half a mile back along the road. Feats like this, and many others, were comparable to fit riders scrapping in open competition. They also provided fairly substantial proof that the JACK KNIFE position was not wrong. At first I experienced leg ache from this machine due to the change in position from the 69 deg. of my immediately previous machine to the 65 deg. seat tube of this experimental model. Evidently the difference was sufficiently great to bring another set of muscles into play. For a time upturned handlebars were used but this appeared to place more body weight upon the saddle and less on the handlebar. The result was that saddlesoreness was experienced on long journeys. Another interesting fact was that the front tyre wore away each side of the tread leaving a ridge untouched in the centre. I thought that this was due to the excessively flexible nature of the fork blades which possibly caused drag of the front wheel as it moved sideways during the process of bounce control, the consequent friction between tyre and road causing the wear. I imagined that this condition was aggravated by the upturned handlebars with the high control point causing more sideways drag than would the lower control point of a dropped bar. A comparison may be drawn between the position of the handlebars and the movement of a flower vase when pushed across a table. If one pushes the vase at the base, it will be found to travel quite steadily, but if the vase is pushed from the top it will tend to tilt and rock when pushed. Thus, with the high point of control on the handlebar position, tilt, drag and sideways movement will be accentuated. On this machine, I was able to carry loads exceeding two hundredweight

with no loss of control at all and with slight extra effort called for on hills. The long rear triangle allowed the weight to be carried in front of the rear wheel spindle, thus avoiding the possibility of a fulcrum occurring at this point—a tendency noticed when weights are carried behind the rear wheel centre. Many readers will appreciate this fact if they have attempted to carry a load supported on a carrier at the rear of a bicycle.

In 1936, my son, Noel, graduated from a toy motor to a two-wheel bicycle which I built and equipped to my own design. The size of the frame was 14in. and was fitted with 14in. wheels. The head angle was 75 deg. combined with a fork offset of 1½in. The seat tube angle was 68 deg. in relation to the ground. The front C to C measurement allowed ample toe clearance and the rear triangle was relatively quite short. The cranks were shortened to 3½in. and the B.B. height was only 7in. Wooden blocks were fitted to the pedals and the gear was 28in. fixed wheel. The handlebars were of the flat type with the grips bent at right angles towards the riding position.

Little progress was made for the first few months as the machine was rather too large for him, making the control difficult. After the wooden pedal blocks were removed and he grew more into the machine great strides in progress were made, and Noel became the fastest pavement cyclist for miles around and soon acquired speeds of twenty miles per hour and even more. The wide angle between head and seat tubes proved very useful because the handlebars and saddle became further apart as they were heightened. As Noel grew and became more accustomed to the machine, a higher gear was fitted and handlebars of the comfort type were fitted, giving considerably more reach and greater knee clearance.

When Noel was 10½ years of age, the war was well in progress and therefore supplies were difficult and new cycles quite out of the question. I therefore fixed up my disused polo cycle for his use, which had a frame with 68 deg. head angle with straight fork blades and 66 deg. seat tube. This bicycle had a 21in. C to C measurement and a 16in. rear triangle, the cranks were 6in. long and the B.B. height was 11in. with 26in. wheels. The rear was raised for normal purposes to 52in. fixed wheel. The frame of this machine was made with tandem fittings and weighed very heavily but despite this Noel rode this machine with great success and learned many lessons in the art of controlling a bicycle.

Towards the end of the war I designed a new machine for my son with a 68 deg. head angle in combination with a 2¼in. fork offset. The seat tube angle was 66 deg. and the top tube length was 21in. The front C to C was 22½in. and that of the rear triangle 19½in. This was virtually a JACK KNIFE bicycle and Noel rode it well although, as he was still a schoolboy, he achieved nothing spectacular, but he was becoming more and more

APPENDIX C

cycle conscious and in particular displayed tremendous interest in the new-found JACK KNIFE position. In the meantime, I was still developing the idea and was in possession of another experimental frame, which eventually became spare. The angles of this machine were precisely the same as those of Noel's but the front C to C was cut down to 22in. and the top tube C to C was 20¼in. while the rear triangle was longer than his own and measured 20¼in. C to C. Noel was keen to try this frame and, after convincing his mother that his toes would never catch the front wheel, gained permission to do so. He transferred all the parts from his old machine to this new frame.

Noel's enthusiasm grew. He saved his money and bought high pressure wheels and tyres. At Christmas, 1947, he was given a present of wooden sprint wheels and tubular tyres, and at the age of sixteen years and one week he ventured on his first 25 mile test ride and did very well. He enjoyed the thrill of this and was promised that he should be allowed to ride again later. During the waiting period before the next try-out Noel decided to have this frame re-enamelled, and while he was waiting for this work to be completed he rode my old wartime experimental relic with wheel-base measuring 48in. He used this for some weeks until, with the next trial date fast approaching, he was able to change back to the original frame which now looked smart and new. He rode this for the next two weeks or so until, within one week of the next trial date, he suddenly said to me, "You know, Dad, I think I could do better on the old trailer bike,"—as we fondly called the old machine. After many protests from his mother about the disgracefulness of the old bike in comparison with the smartness of his newly-enamelled machine he eventually gained his own way, and three days before the next test he fixed it up with sprints and tubulars. So it came about that he rode his next test ride on 48in. of wheel-base. The machine included in its specification a pannier carrier welded solidly to the seat stays upon which in the old days Noel himself had often been carried, with Dad as stoker. The frame, to this day, has never been filed and has only been painted by hand with house paint. In this ride, Noel's time improved by 1½ minutes.

Noel was really encouraged by this result and, having given a good account of himself, was in effect asking for more. The JACK KNIFE position was in his blood and he wanted to help develop the idea still further.

After much discussion we together decided on a new frame design for Noel. This design is shown in detail in diagram 8. We intended in this design to exaggerate the JACK KNIFE principles to the utmost proportions practicable. We had by us an old chain-wheel set with 48-teeth chain-wheel and cranks 5¼in. long. This was a relic of another earlier experiment. By using this we could cut the front C to C still shorter but we agreed to leave the rear triangle at not more than 26in. as this would already be propor-

tionately longer than the back of the old machine in view of the shorter front C to C measurement. Noel rode this machine intent on the utmost indulgence to JACK KNIFE principles. That is, with seat position well behind the B.B., short top tube and low handlebars. The seat position was brought forward as close as possible to the front wheel leaving the rear wheel stable and well back so as to follow through, as he had now learned he could depend upon it to do, in any emergency. Not content with this, Noel later approached me about the prospect of pushing his saddle still further back. The only way to do this was to make and fit a backwardly-pointing seat pin. This we did, making the backward-pointing portion 4in. long. A few days later, to my great surprise, I noticed that his saddle was perched on the extreme end of the rear-pointing tube. The angle of the seat tube was already 65 deg. so the saddle fixing clip being 4in. behind the centre of this meant that the aggregate seat tube angle was 55 deg. in relation to the ground. (This calculation being based on the scale of ⅜in. of movement equalling 1 deg.) Noel insisted that this was most comfortable and that he would not mind pushing the saddle still further back. I regarded the good sense of this development with suspicion for I thought his enthusiasm was outstripping his better judgment. However, Noel insisted and meanwhile a third 25-mile test, for which he had entered, was due. This he rode after less than two weeks' use of this new machine and with the saddle position as described. He again used his sprints but, in view of the 5¼in. crank length, the gear was lowered from 76in., as previously used, to 69in. for his third attempt. His time was 36 seconds slower than his previous best, and although he finished fresh he suffered considerable saddle soreness. He did not ride again for the next two days and when he did venture out the rear-ward-pointing seat pin had been replaced by the original straight one.

Noel has not attempted another test since this ride as most of his time has been absorbed in assisting with the launching of our enterprise known as Frederick H. Pratt & Son. Also he is only a lad, and common sense suggests that he should not be allowed to over tax his strength. In spite of his limited spare time Noel has ridden this new machine of his quite considerably. Noel and I have been watching and noting every reaction as he has been subjecting this cycle to various treatments, and one thing which we have found of particular interest is that his front tyre has shown signs of wear on each side of the tread, leaving a distinct unworn ridge down the centre, in the same way that had happened to my early experimental model. In order to trace the source of this trouble I had followed Noel in a car watching his every movement. Wag does occur sometimes. One time when it occurs is occasionally at the commencement of an up gradient and more frequently when pedalling downhill without forward pressure using a fixed wheel. After close and careful study we have proved to our satisfaction that it is confined to the front of the machine and that the unusual tyre wear in both cases was due

APPENDIX C

to presence of wag and not to the set of conditions given in the earlier part of this discussion. Noel has used exceedingly low handlebars and on all occasions the grips have, in fact, been lower than the front fork crown.

There is a distinct difference between the kind of wag experienced on the exaggerated upright design to that found with the exaggerated JACK KNIFE position. On the upright machine the whole back part wobbles or waves from side to side, the axis of movement being through a vertical line somewhere near the front of the machine and it appears most probable that it occurs through the point where the hands grip the handlebars, but on the exaggerated JACK KNIFE position the axis of movement is through the front tyre where it is in contact with the ground. The rider and the top portion of the machine provide the movement by tending to heave from side to side in rhythm with the pedal rotation as the machine is being held in check. This wagging does not always occur where Noel and his extra long back JACK KNIFE position are concerned. When he has his mind on keeping steady the machine never deviates from the perpendicular and he then rides with unusual precision.

Another difficulty which Noel has come up against is the presence of wheel spin. He has lost quite a lot of tread from his rear tyre through this and it is found to occur particularly when hill climbing. I never found this difficulty with my long-base machine No. 1 and I suppose that I did not push hard enough, but it was noticed that my rear wheel locked readily when braking.

In passing, there is another type, or style, of machine of which the reader may be thinking. This is the recumbent position, but, in case some readers are not familiar with this type of machine I will briefly explain what it is. The rider lies on his back between two much smaller than usual road wheels and the pedals are usually positioned just behind the front wheel and drive the rear wheel through a long transmission comprising one or more series of chain and chain-wheels. The front wheel steering is connected by rods to a handlebar arrangement which comes out to grips, one on each side of the rider. This position gives considerable advantage to the power push of the legs and pull of the arms as the legs are directly in compression and the arms in direct tension. The push and pull take place in one and the same straight line. The rider's back in turn presses hard against an inclined back-rest which adds still more power to the legs by placing the body as well as the legs in compression. Added to this a still further tremendous advantage exists in that the rider is travelling feet first and is practically flat on his back so that wind resistance is reduced to negligible proportions. Riders of these machines can acquire speeds unheard of with orthodox bicycles and we have proof of this because many long-standing records have been decisively shattered by second-rate riders on recumbent bicycles. These outstanding feats however are not convincing proof of the practicability of this type of machine and none of these records are recognised officially. The fact is that these machines are dangerous. In traffic, the rider, being so low, is overshadowed by the other traffic and the danger of being run down is considerable as they cannot be seen by other road users. A still more condemning feature is that the rider cannot see where he is going and also the machine is very fatiguing to ride at all times.

My personal experience with the use of upright angled machines is not extensive, the most upright seat angle I have tried is 72 deg. This I did not ride successfully, but just tolerated. I find seats up to 70 deg. tolerable and that comfort departs when more upright than 68 deg. I have, there is no doubt, trained myself against steep angles and this is probably the reason why I have difficulty in using them. My prejudice is probably due to lack of faith in these principles, having observed the shortcomings of others who more blithely indulge in the practise. I suggest that the increased number of accidents on our tracks are caused by upright angles in combination with short rear triangles. Sprinters, because of the difficulty in controlling such machines, wobble excessively, and, should another rider venture too close, there is invariably an accident. Riders of this class of machine are the best judges of the accuracy of this statement.

I quite honestly deplore upright designs when carried to extreme but am only stubborn about my views because nobody has, as yet, produced sufficient proof to alter these views. I persist in my arguments because I sincerely believe in my views and think that I can help others by passing on the knowledge. Unlike my predecessors I endeavour to supply reasons for any recommendation made, and the quality of the reasons can then indicate the value of my advice. As new facts become unfolded I shall mould my views, contradicting previous statements where this becomes necessary. My son and I, as a firm, will learn as we teach and teach as we learn. We learn by teaching, as our motto indicates.

Now let us sum up our observations in this fourth leaflet. Diagram No. 1 features the JACK KNIFE position in its most severe practical form. Here the weight of the rider is correctly distributed between the two wheels, the angle between the power of the arms and legs is closed to a desirable minimum, the head angle and fork offset provide excellent conditions for bounce control, making the presence of front wheel toe overlap tolerable and even desirable where maximum speed is the object. Whilst the dimensions are not fixed or binding it provides a basis upon which to work from the JACK KNIFE position to the most extreme upright-angled designs. To exaggerate this basic design far beyond the agreed reasonable proportions as we have done in our efforts to prove its worth causes disadvantages mainly due to the fact that the 26in. long C to C rear triangle places the rider's weight relatively too far forward, with the result that the influence of the rider's movements are centred too much on the front wheel. In

APPENDIX C

the event of weight-carrying, such as that of camping equipment, no other arrangement could be more desirable. The load positioned as explained in my description of experiences of long-base machine No. 1 holds the rear wheel down and provides the necessary steadying agent so making the weight distribution even once more, removing the unbalanced load from the front wheel as experienced when riding light.

Amongst our discoveries we also found that the rider can be seated too far back and that there is a point where the saddle appears to position the rider on a point of balance between tilting forward and backward. We believe that the true facts of the case are as follows: when the rider's weight is in front of this point of balance the power of the arms tends to pull the rider forward from the saddle, conversely, when it is positioned behind this point the power of the arms then tends to increase the downward pressure of the body on the saddle. The latter condition increases as fatigue overtakes the rider. We would advise that the rider endeavours to find a position where his weight is correctly balanced, that is, a position in equilibrium between the power pull of the arms and the push of the legs. He can then use his strength to full advantage without feeling the tendency to be pulled forward or experiencing undue pressure on the saddle. A further back position therefore lends itself more to the purpose of short sprints than to rides of longer duration where fatigue tends to lessen the rider's live weight on the pedals.

On the other hand, there is no alternative course than to drift by degrees from the arrangement of diagram No. 1 towards that of diagram No. 7. In keeping with our beliefs that there is nothing more suitable when drawing comparisons than to exaggerate them we have produced in diagram No. 7 a highly exaggerated upright form of machine. To be scientifically correct this layout is provided with a very shallow fork offset with the purpose of avoiding rise and fall of the front of the machine when steered. The down tube is of extreme length and the front C to C measurement also unnecessarily long, but these conditions must prevail in view of the fact that if either of the measurements were less then the down tube would encroach upon the clearance necessary to allow the front wheel to turn. The rear triangle is drawn as short as possible, as is consistent with the demands of this type of machine, and in keeping with the usual short wheel-bases found on these types.

Diagram No. 8 may, perhaps, appear absurd when judged upon the accepted standards of the present day but we leave it to the reader to decide whether diagram No. 7 or 8 is the more absurd. Both are exaggerated versions of what they are intended to represent.

Returning once more to diagram No. 1 we would emphasize that this is the design which we recommend as the best arrangement for the purpose of utmost speed. Diagrams Nos. 2, 3 and 4 showing gradual modifications bring peace of mind to those who suspect danger in front wheel toe overlap but we must remind those readers that the diagrams represent the first steps on the way towards the conditions existing in diagram No. 7.

On many occasions we hear comments that more upright angles are required for track racing than for road use. We ask "Why?". On the contrary, we recommend more upright angles for touring purposes as this provides the desirable toe clearance usually requested by the tourist. This condition is achieved by increasing the front C to C measurement without shifting the saddle back unduly, so avoiding incorrect distribution of body-weight between the two road wheels. Diagrams No. 5 and 6 according to this theory are more suitable for leisure purposes but this is not actually true since they represent several stages nearer to the conditions of diagram No. 7. The real purpose of their existence is to provide the necessary stepping stones from extreme upright angles to the JACK KNIFE position.

We hope sincerely that in the presentation of this series of leaflets we are being of service to our readers.

Once a lad with time on hand
Desired to travel o'er the land.
First he tarried on a hike,
Then his thoughts turned to a bike.
Steep head, long reach, all continental,
Bright paint and gadgets ornamental.
He rode well but had to rest,
The handlebars were never best,
Pedal place not just so,
Best attempts were always slow.
Anxious to improve condition
He tried a bike JACK KNIFE position.
He first attempted with a thrill
The THRUSTING ACTION up a hill,
Over the top with grand success
From UPWARD LIFT to DOWNWARD PRESS.
A scrapping crowd was next attraction,
He passed them all with CAT'S CLAW ACTION.

FREDERICK H. PRATT.

APPENDIX

JACK KNIFE DESIGN	HEAD ANGLE	FORK OFFSET	SEAT ANGLE	TOP TUBE C to C	FRONT C to C	REAR TRIANGLE
Diagram No. 1	71	$2\frac{1}{4}$	66	$22\frac{1}{8}$	$21\frac{7}{8}$	$21\frac{1}{2}$
2	71	$2\frac{1}{4}$	67	$22\frac{3}{8}$	$22\frac{1}{2}$	$20\frac{7}{8}$
3	71	$2\frac{1}{4}$	68	$22\frac{5}{8}$	$23\frac{1}{8}$	$20\frac{1}{4}$
4	71	$2\frac{1}{4}$	69	$22\frac{7}{8}$	$23\frac{3}{4}$	$19\frac{5}{8}$
JACK KNIFE DESIGN APPLIED						
Diagram No. 5	75	$1\frac{13}{16}$	71	$22\frac{3}{4}$	$22\frac{1}{2}$	$18\frac{7}{8}$
Recommended modification of						
Diagram No. 5	75	$2\frac{1}{4}$	71	$22\frac{1}{4}$	$22\frac{1}{2}$	$19\frac{1}{2}$
Diagram No. 6	75	$1\frac{13}{16}$	73	$23\frac{1}{4}$	$23\frac{3}{4}$	$17\frac{1}{2}$
Recommended modification of						
Diagram No. 6	75	$2\frac{1}{4}$	73	$22\frac{3}{4}$	$23\frac{3}{4}$	$18\frac{1}{2}$

APPENDIX B

The above table can serve as a catalogue, presenting the dimensions of all diagrams at a glance. Frame designs can be ordered by stating the required diagram number. Prices are available on application, the decorative finishes in particular influence these. All frames are built with the finest grade high tensile materials obtainable, by skilled hands guided by purposeful brains, so making the product comparable to a Strad. violin.

The most desirable commodities are not yet available, but, with the possibility of obtaining specially made parts, in the not too distant future, new and novel methods of frame construction will be adopted. Until then we will continue to do our best with the best parts procurable. As stated in the body of this leaflet, I have very definite views about cycle construction, and apart from the shapes which have already been dealt with, I make the following additional suggestions. In theory, by laboratory tests, bronze welded construction is stronger than a socketed joint brazed by capillary attraction, but my experience has taught me that lug sockets, in effect, shorten the distance from joint to joint and thereby render the frame less whippy.

When lugs are available we shall build lugged frames, with sockets left as long as possible but cut away sufficiently to avoid a sudden change of section at the joints and we shall leave the maximum length of metal on the sides to support the tubes against lateral whip. Large diameter tubes of lighter gauge will always be favoured, and in the event of welded construction extra large diameter tubes will be embodied in an effort to compensate for the lack of lug support. We also favour the use of D-section forks, for I have proof that these are the strongest possible. Like most things appertaining to bicycles, statements such as these involve many questions and require lengthy explanations in their justification. This leaflet does not allow space for this, therefore they must be the subject of some future publication which may be entirely given up to their consideration.

APPENDIX C

Children & Bicycles
by Frederick Pratt

A bicycle is good fun for children, if they own one they always have something to do.

A bicycle makes your child responsible, he becomes expert and learns road sense.

A child will sometimes fall off, if he does he will be more careful not to repeat the experience, this is process of learning.

One day your child will drive a car. He will do it, regardless of his parents' wishes. If he has ridden a cycle as a small boy, this experience will help him to cope with the problem of driving safely.

If your child has never had the privilege of owning a cycle at an early age, he will be just as foolish on the road at 12 or 13 years old, as the child of 4 years when he started ~~careless road~~.

Riding a bicycle is healthy exercise, you use your legs with the weight off your feet.

You can make cycling as easy or as hard as you wish, by fitting the appropriate gear ratios. A dropped handlebar streamlines the rider, adds purchase to his strength and provides change of position by many holding points. The more you ride your cycle the easier it becomes.

A bicycle will soon earn its keep, saving fares on public transport.

A bicycle only deteriorates prematurely when it is allowed to rust.

Bent forks, & pedals can be straightened, wheels can be trued, a pair of new mudguards costs but a few shillings, and will smarten things up surprisingly.

There is always a secondhand demand for bicycles out-grown, a new cycle for your child is NOT money thrown away.

Call and see FREDERICK PRATT & SON, they will supply the right machine to set you or your child on the road to happy cycling.

32 BRIGHTON RD. SALFORDS, NR. REDHILL.
Tel. Horley 5165

The Lynn Shaw Press, Woodhatch Road, Redhill, Surrey.

Cyclists!

Have you read the following really helpful and instructive pamphlets?

1. THE JACK-KNIFE POSITION.
2. PEDALLING A BICYCLE EFFICIENTLY.
3. THE PROGRESS OF DESIGN.

This series is of real use to the enthusiastic rider, whether he be a racing man or a "potterer" with a wish for increased mileage without extra effort!

SEND A POSTAL ORDER FOR 10d. NOW

AND MAKE SURE OF YOUR COPIES

By return of Post from :

FREDERICK H. PRATT & SON,
BRIGHTON ROAD, SALFORDS, SURREY.

APPENDIX C